Walt Disney's

A TRUE-LIFE ADVENTURE

WORLDS OF NATURE

A TREASURY OF TRUE-LIFE ADVENTURES

WALT DISNEY'S

WORLDS OF NATURE

BY RUTHERFORD PLATT
and the Staff
of the WALT DISNEY STUDIO

Based on the Walt Disney
Motion Picture Series
TRUE-LIFE ADVENTURES

GOLDEN PRESS • NEW YORK

Contents

FOREWORD . . . . *page* 10

The Arctic Wonderland 12

The Mountain Stronghold 44

Prairie Horizons 70

Desert Miracles 82

Big Adventures in Little Worlds 94

The Big Swamp 150

Mysterious Africa 162

INDEX 176

Foreword

The pages of this book will lead you into seven worlds of wonder, each one more marvelous than any fairy-tale kingdom ever dreamed of by man. The seven worlds of wonder are areas of our earth's crust where nature is supreme: mountains, forests, prairies, deserts, swamps, seas, and icecaps.

If you were on the moon peering through a telescope at our planet, you would see these regions flashing with ever-changing colors from the spinning earth. According to the changing seasons and the varying angles of light between sunrise and sunset, the regions would appear to be green, yellow, black, red, brown, blue, white. Man's cities would be mere specks; the places where he has destroyed the face of nature would be almost invisible, while the seven worlds of wonder would shine with beauty.

Nobody could ever guess, looking at the earth through a telescope on the moon, what strange and wonderful creatures hide in each tantalizing place. Even we, who share the same planet with them, have taken a long time to discover some of these creatures.

Until recent times, people thought that life could not exist in the deep freeze of the Polar North, and in the scorched sands of the desert. Not until the middle of the last century did man explore the interior of Africa, which remained such a mystery that it was called the "dark continent." Even the depths of the wonderful worlds within worlds around us were not well known. Nature's near-by half acre and the living miracles inside ponds and swamps kept their secrets. Then in recent years came new kinds of lenses, photographic techniques, and forms of transportation that have helped us to cross frontiers and bring back, for all to see, the drama of life in strange places.

There is high adventure in the strange kingdoms where huge giants and unbelievably small dwarfs pursue life in their peculiar ways. Each world of wonder has its own kinds of plants and animals, and each kind fits its place, whether that be as big as a savanna or as little as a drop of water, as hot as a desert or as cold as an iceberg, as wet as an ocean wave or as dry as a sun-bathed rock, as dark as a tunnel or as bright as a mountain top.

The creatures that live in such varied places differ widely in size and in body mechanisms. There are giant lions and elephants, medium-sized bears and birds, little spiders and bees, and animals so tiny that you cannot see them with

the naked eye. All these beings have two things in common: they are all subject to the same laws of nature, and they all get their power from the sun.

To make this book about the wonders of life would have been impossible a few years ago. Today we can bring it to you with photographs that show in their true colors the worlds of nature and the fantastic creatures that dwell in those worlds. Some of the creatures are as beautiful as music, others as ugly as dragons; some are fierce and brutal, others delicate and gentle. They are caught in moments of attack and escape, of fun and family life, of stalking and pouncing and swooping and swimming. Most of the photographs are the fruit of ten years of exploration by a few devoted people, who, armed with new and unusual camera equipment and inexhaustible patience, created our True-Life Adventure films: *Arctic Wilderness, Bear Country, Seal Island, Beaver Valley, Olympic Elk, Vanishing Prairie, Living Desert, Nature's Half Acre, Secrets of Life, Prowlers of the Everglades, Water Birds,* and *African Lion.* These twelve films form the foundation of the book you are about to read.

Walt Disney

Credits

The photographs in this book were taken by:

RUTHERFORD PLATT
ALFRED G. MILOTTE
JAMES R. SIMON
WARREN E. GARST
HUGH A. WILMAR
ROBERT H. CRANDALL
STUART V. JEWELL
EDWARD B. PRIMS
GEORGE A. PRIMS
N. PAUL KENWORTHY, JR.
TOM MC HUGH
ART RILEY
MARY CARRICK
HERB CRISLER
ALFRED HOLZ
ROY EDWARD DISNEY
CLEVELAND P. GRANT
FRAN WILLIAM HALL
MARY WILMAR
SARASOTA JUNGLE GARDENS, FLORIDA
AMERICAN MUSEUM OF NATURAL HISTORY
MAC'S PHOTO SERVICE, ANCHORAGE, ALASKA
FOUKE FUR CO.
CLAUDE JENDRUSCH
FLORIDA STATE NEWS BUREAU
HENRY B. KANE
JOSEF MUENCH
LLOYD BEEBE
FRED KOPIETZ
R. C. AND CLAIRE MEYER PROCTOR
MURL DEUSING
CECIL RHODE
TILDEN W. ROBERTS
OLIN SEWALL PETTINGILL, JR.
ARTHUR S. CARTER
NORBERT WITKOWSKY
CAMERA CLIX
HAWAII NATURAL HISTORY ASSOCIATION
MILWAUKEE PUBLIC MUSEUM
DR. VINCENT SCHAEFER

The drawings in this book are by Paula Hutchison, Art Riley, Joshua Meador, and Campbell Grant.

In the faint, eerie light of the arctic sun, a polar bear cub climbs onto a floating ice pan, looking for fish for his supper.

The Arctic Wonderland

In this fantastic land the sun rises once a year. At that moment the drama of life, awakening out of frozen seas, raw rocks, and bitter winds, is enacted on a grand scale. A few weeks earlier a red glow appeared over the southern horizon, dimming the aurora borealis, whose streamers had shed an unearthly white light for months over an utterly silent, motionless, and apparently dead landscape. The red glow had been gradually getting brighter until, at the moment of the beginning of our story, a flaming disk suddenly slid above the horizon.

On the first day the disk seems to hesitate before so great a task as warming up an empire of ice, where the thermometer stands at 60 degrees below zero. It does not rise above a half circle before it sinks back, to become a bright spot like a huge bonfire at the edge of the sea. Then again it glides up with a momentum that carries it into the clear in all its roundness. At this moment sunrise and sunset are combined into one event—and the grip of the long polar night is broken! The empire of ice will be shattered by sunlight.

During the weeks that follow, great miracles occur. Continuous darkness is replaced by continuous light. The sun goes around and around the horizon without setting. Instead of an unbroken flat expanse of whiteness, brittle as glass and hard as steel, patches of deep blue water appear, widening and sparkling in the sunlight. Instead of utter silence (for even the great winds of the north pour through space in silence, there being no trees or buildings or wires to make them roar and whistle) there is the grinding and crackling of ice, the splashing of water falling off cliffs, the barking of seals, the squawking of countless birds. Back of all

The great hole in this towering iceberg was made by an underground river that flowed through the part of the glacier where the ice was forming.

The top of the world, still in the Ice Age, is an untouched wilderness of nature. Every year numberless birds and animals invade it to reach their breeding grounds. And here on the arctic tundras grow some of the healthiest and most colorful wildflowers found anywhere in the world.

these local sounds the deep voice of the polar region can be heard. This is the sound of unlocking glaciers and icebergs when tensions deep within the ice are released by the warmth of the sun. Usually the sound is heard across a vast distance like the booming of faraway thunder. Close by it is appalling. This wild booming occurs when a big iceberg is calved at the face of a glacier, or when an iceberg afloat suddenly explodes into a million pieces.

The miraculous strangeness of the arctic is heightened when the sun shines from due south at noon, then circles around to shine from due north at midnight. There is no frost or dew, no moon or stars—there is just immense space made out of sea, rock, ice, and snow. Without familiar objects like trees or buildings for comparison, it is impossible to judge distance or size. A huge iceberg looks like a speck, a tremendous cliff looks easy to climb, a roaring torrent cutting a canyon looks like a silver thread, a pile of boulders with rocks up to ten feet in diameter looks like an ordinary sand dune. Islands and mountains shrink; they seem almost as small as those on a map. The space of the arctic is continuous with the space of the sky. This is the greatest untouched wilderness of nature on the face of the earth.

WORLD OF FLOWERS

Bleak monotony is not the truth, or the whole truth, about this land.

All over the arctic and right up to the edge of the Polar Sea are scattered some of the healthiest, most freely blooming, and brightly colored wildflowers in the world. They include fireweed, poppy, saxifrage, mustard, arctic rose, chickweed, and bluebells. They grow so fast

that they fairly explode out of the ground after the sunrise in April, and bloom vigorously all summer. In a land where everything is on such an immense scale, arctic plants are miniatures. They do not cover the ground except in patches, but they are scattered in cracks of granite and snuggle under boulders. There are no trees as we think of trees, but birch, poplar, and willow grow as flat as though a steam roller had ironed them out. These strange trees are able to collect a great deal of sunlight because they are only a few inches in height and spread out widely. As there is no fertile soil, they make their own soil out of their brown leaves of previous years, which pile up at the top of the root, where they hold moisture and sun warmth.

AN ICE-AGE ANIMAL

With such a wealth of plants in the arctic wonderland there should also be animals, and there are. Yet we only half-believe that any animal can live where the musk ox lives. This beast, which belongs in the storybook of prehistoric monsters, really exists—we can hear it snort and see its wool, three feet long, waving in the arctic winds. This living monument of the Ice Age, ragged and humped up, does not run and jump gracefully like a deer, but clumps along on stumpy legs. It looks like a crazy combination of a bull and an oversized sheep. Most of the time it is patient and friendly; but when danger threatens, it bucks and kicks.

Musk ox, with its big shaggy head turned toward the ground like an American buffalo's, pays no attention to the millions of birds that come to its country to nest in the spring. And in the summertime there is plenty of room in the numberless arctic valleys for both caribou and musk ox; so they do not war on each other.

When the caribou troop southward in the fall to where trees give hospitable shelter at the edge of the open tundra, the musk ox turns in the opposite direction. It moves up into the mountains where the cruel gales, which would freeze almost any other animal to death in five

In mid-winter, a hungry tundra wolf stalks his prey along a desolate, snowbound river.

At the head of a rugged fjord on the coast of Greenland, a glacier meets the sea. Here huge icebergs are "calved" when, with a roar and a crash, they split off the dazzling ice face and plunge into the water.

minutes, keep the ground clear of snow. It saunters to the northernmost point of land in the world—Cape Morris Jessup, only 380 miles from the North Pole. There, in the winter, the animal munches serenely on dead plants, frozen berries, and woolly lichens, to keep its blood warm through the fury of the polar night.

In the desolation and loneliness of mid-winter, the musk ox lives undisturbed. Its natural enemy, the white wolf, has learned—the hard way—to respect a herd of musk oxen. The herd backs together, big heads facing out, to form a hollow square like the military formations of old wars. Cows and babies take their places in the center, or sometimes young calves get under the bellies of the bulls and hide behind their woolly curtains.

And now, while waiting for the wolf to charge, the oxen do a strange thing. They stoop down and rub their heads against their forelegs. A powerful odor from scent glands just below each eye is released; it carries three hundred feet beyond the formation. The purpose of this scent is a mystery. It may be to warn an enemy of trouble ahead, as does a skunk, or perhaps it is a means of rousing good-natured animals to action. At the first whiff the musk ox is transformed into a nimble, aggressive animal. It charges out swiftly, gives a swipe with its horns—murderous blades that curve down and then up — and then backs quickly into formation.

If a musk ox is grabbed by a wolf, he bucks and kicks like a steer in a rodeo, then leaps and, turning in the air, crashes down on his side to crush the wolf. If the wolf or any other offending animal stumbles or is trapped, the musk ox will gore and trample and fling the miserable creature to death. But all this is pure defense, for the musk ox, living in a country where there is very little prey, gets all the food he needs from the small arctic plants.

This lonely animal that thrives in the land of the midnight sun has a protective coloring. The shaggy fur is mottled with dark colors, with black spots below, so that when the animal stands still in the light of the summer sun it blends with boulders. From a short distance it is almost invisible. A stroke of genius in the camouflage is a patch of white on the broad back and high saddle—a perfect imitation of a boulder with snow on top! Perhaps this effective camouflage is left over from the time when the musk ox had the company of many other animals which have since vanished from the earth.

About 20,000 years ago, a sheet of ice some two miles deep buried Canada and reached down into the United States nearly as far as Cincinnati and St. Louis. The western mountains of our land were buried in vast ice fields. Musk oxen grazed across the snowy plains in front of the glaciers, where Kansas and Pennsylvania are today. With them were reindeer, wolves, mammoths, and many other animals. But as the climate of the world grew milder, the glaciers melted back and retreated over the northern horizon. The glaciers in the western

During the short summer season, the cinquefoil plant produces a single delicate blossom.

Brilliant clumps of yellow cinquefoil and white saxifrage grow in rocky crevices on the tundra.

Lichen plants paint barren rocks with warm colors.

mountains shrank up into the highest valleys and ravines, and forests soon covered the slopes. This marvelous transformation took place in a few thousand years, and left the world as we see it. The woolly mammoths and the mastodons, perhaps too big and clumsy to keep moving with the times, died out. The mountain goats, which enjoy rocks, ice, and snow, advanced to the mountain tops. Foxes, rabbits, wolves, caribou, and polar bears followed the retreating ice sheet.

The musk ox, with its rare formula for living, has kept its place right in the middle of the Ice Age through the thousands of years. It has the hollow-square defense and self-rousing battle odor against its one natural enemy, the white wolf. It is easygoing and doesn't rush around frantically getting into trouble. It can live simply on the tiny plants under its feet, whether fresh or frozen. And in a country where it is impossible to dig a lair, it can stand out in the full force of a gale, in intense cold, blanketed by those efficient woolly curtains.

As the arctic summer melts glaciers and snow, and the land is uncovered, flowers and grasses spring up, advancing as far as the edge of the wall of ice.

BIGGEST EVER

While the musk ox is the great land survivor of the ancient Ice Age, the ancestors of some animals of today were disporting themselves in the oceans of the last Ice Age—and millions of years before that.

The sea has always been an easier place to live than land. World-wide ocean currents keep the temperature of sea water fairly even. Even when the sea freezes over, the ice crust averages only four feet thick—maximum seven feet—and underneath that crust is plenty of water with temperatures well above freezing. An animal can become a giant in the sea, moreover, and still travel easily. The body of a whale need not be suspended from its backbone, as in land animals. The water around the whale, not the backbone, holds up its great weight. The whale can move its tonnage by simply floating with the currents, or swimming with a lazy flip of a fluke. The sea, like the air, allows its creatures to move in all directions and travel long distances at will; swimming and gliding under water are similar to flying and soaring as ways of going places without much effort.

The largest monster on record was not reconstructed out of fossil bones millions of years old: it was a blue whale, caught in 1948. This animal weighed one hundred fifty tons, as compared to fifty tons for the biggest known dinosaur, and it was almost ninety feet long. Such whales are also the animals that pack the greatest power. One harpooned whale towed a whaling steamer (with engines going full speed astern) at eight miles per hour for seven hours before it tired. It must have been capable of about four hundred horsepower to do that.

No big animal in the world is so fortunate as the whale in getting food. An elephant needs a square mile of jungle to keep its stomach filled, and the square miles of jungle are shrinking. But whales today have seas as vast as they ever were. When the cruising blue whale opens its mouth wide, a few thousand gallons of water pour through the rows of whalebone hanging from

Musk oxen live closer to the North Pole than any other land animals. Protected by their shaggy warm wool coats, they can withstand the coldest arctic winters.

the upper jaw. These strain out tiny shrimp (called krill), herring, and countless other kinds of seafood. The strained water is jettisoned (a whale doesn't drink salt water) while the seafood goes down the throat. The gullet will not pass anything bigger than herring, but a whale can still enjoy a ton of fish chowder per meal.

Whales in their present form have lived in the sea for some 25 million years. Before that, for more millions of years, their ancestors were running around on land. When the climate changed and there was not enough food on land, these animals took to the sea. Other land animals were the ancestors of seals, dolphins, walruses, and other warm-blooded mammals.

The whale is not a fish. The front flippers are forelegs and still have five fingers, though now the front flippers are used only to keep the whale from rolling over, and to help steer. The whale is propelled by huge horizontal tail flukes, which are flapped up and down by very powerful muscles, as one sculls with an oar at the rear of a boat. The whale's hind limbs have disappeared except for one leg bone, about ten inches long, buried in the body and no longer attached to the backbone.

The whale lives comfortably in cold water without getting chilled, because its frame is covered with an enormous layer of fat, as much as twelve inches thick, called blubber. Blubber also makes the whale buoyant. To dive, the whale must use its tail flukes.

Blubber also is an elastic covering that helps the whale's body to bear the enormous underwater pressures when he dives deep. A whale can go down 3,200 feet. The pressure at that depth is almost a hundred times greater than on the surface, and would crush a blubberless whale.

When wolves attack the musk-ox herd, the adult bulls surround cows and calves, facing out with heads lowered—threatening the enemy with their vicious horns.

A whale takes a breath much as it takes a mouthful of fish broth. From a breathing hole at the highest point of its head, the breathing pipe leads into huge lungs that expand like rubber balloons. When the whale dives, the nostrils close, and the animal can stay down from thirty minutes to an hour.

When the whale surfaces for a breath of fresh air, it lets go with such a giant sneeze that a spout of vapor shoots twenty feet into the air, making a rushing sound which can be heard a mile away. This is not a waterspout, although it looks like that from a distance. It is warm air from the whale's big lung vaporizing when it meets the cold air, as when you "see your breath" on a cold day.

THE LITTLE WHITE WHALES

There are also little whales, ten or fifteen feet long, weighing a ton or so. When summer is in full swing and the arctic ice pack is only "broken white china" scattered along the shore, open blue water is cut by the fins of beautiful white whales. These never travel alone, like their giant relatives. In droves they scoot along just below the surface, the water boiling across their backs. One of the greatest wild animal exhibitions ever witnessed was put on when eight hundred white whales came leaping like a beautiful ballet into the St. Lawrence River.

Such a performance looks gay and carefree. Actually, the whales are going after their dinner—a school of herring. The whales must travel faster than the herring, and dive at terrific speed.

They never collide, never break the beautiful rhythm of the school, never get confused. This amazing co-ordination is possible because of built-in echo-sounding equipment. Lacking external ears, whales have sensitive hearing canals for use under water. Here a school of white whales utters sounds: trilling calls like canaries, rapid clicks, rusty-hinge squeaks, and harsh cheers—their sounds of communication. Sometimes it's like an orchestra tuning up; at other times it sounds like children at play in a distant schoolyard.

THE TRUE UNICORN

A thousand years ago, perhaps, a Viking touring the far arctic ran across the narwhal, forgotten cousin of the whale. He took its horn home and started the legend of the unicorn.

Small compared to a whale, the living unicorn is much larger than the horse on the English coat-of-arms which has the horn com-

At the edge of the Labrador tundra, pipewort can be found growing in shallow pools. The matted, low green growth is the crowberry plant—a favorite food for many of the region's animals and birds.

Vast icebergs float with four-fifths of their bulk submerged in the sea. They are fragments of glaciers, formed as the snows of hundreds of years of blizzards are pressed into ice.

ing out of its forehead. The ash-gray body is flecked with dark spots. Out of the face protrudes the huge spear of spiraling ivory. Few land animals could ever manage such a heavy projection thrust straight out.

The narwhal is lonely but secure in its fiord hideaway. The killer whale doesn't go that far north, and the polar bear concentrates on small seals and baby walruses. No one has ever seen narwhals fencing or whacking at each other with their spears.

Arctic explorers report that the narwhal's spear is fine for catching the animal's favorite food—halibut, a flat fish that rests on the ocean bottom in shallow water. They point out that the spear saves a lot of frantic chasing, snapping, and tussling with the fish. A short sudden thrust, and the halibut is dangling at the tip of the spear. The narwhal now swims straight ahead, and the halibut turns around and around on the spear, moving down the spiral, until it pops into the narwhal's mouth.

WALRUS

The whale is magnificent and imposing; the narwhal is fat, lazy, and lucky to have a spear. What can be said about the walrus, cousin to both of them?

This is another warm-blooded animal of the land which, in the invisible depths of time, turned into a sea animal. It has retained all four limbs, each with five digits. To sit down, the walrus folds its hind legs forward, sits on its haunches, spreads its fore-flippers and leans on them.

It looks like a wise elder statesman, with two drooping tusks two or even three feet long. Small eyes and nostrils are pushed up to the top

The narwhal's long spiral horn does not serve as a weapon. It is used, instead, in spearing fish for dinner.

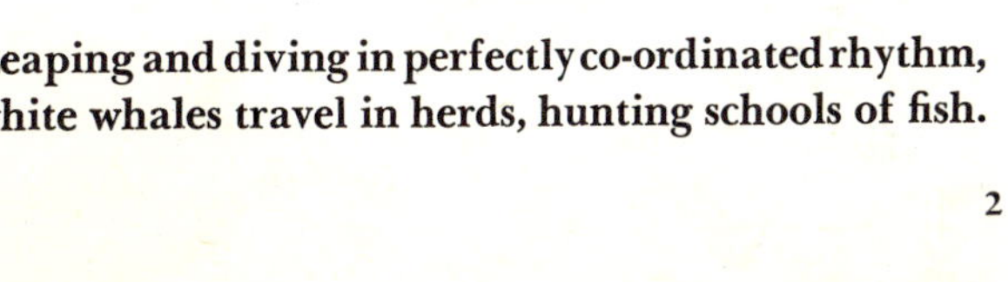

Leaping and diving in perfectly co-ordinated rhythm, white whales travel in herds, hunting schools of fish.

Although walruses are equally at home on floating ice pans, this large herd has come to rest in a rocky cove on the Alaskan shore.

of its head. Its wide muzzles have big, long quills sticking out all over them. Its body, which is almost hairless, is wrapped in huge, ungainly folds of skin.

This monster is certainly one of the ugliest animals on earth, but that is not all. People who have looked into its watery eyes after it has been harpooned see an expression of amazement and disappointment that there is such cruelty in the world.

Those big, drooping tusks are used more energetically than narwhal's spear. When the walrus is hungry, it takes a deep breath and sinks fifty to three hundred feet to the bottom of the sea. Standing on its head, it brings the tusks into a horizontal position to rake up the bottom. It digs out clams, tears mussels off rocks, and rakes up snails, shrimp, starfish, sea-urchins, and anything else on the ocean floor that can't swim away.

The front flippers of the walrus are so short that it cannot use them to push food into the mouth. When the food is raked together in a pile by the tusks, the animal feeds by working the big quills on the muzzle-like fingers.

Walruses travel under water singly like whales and seals, but when they climb out to sleep on ice pans or rock they like to herd to-

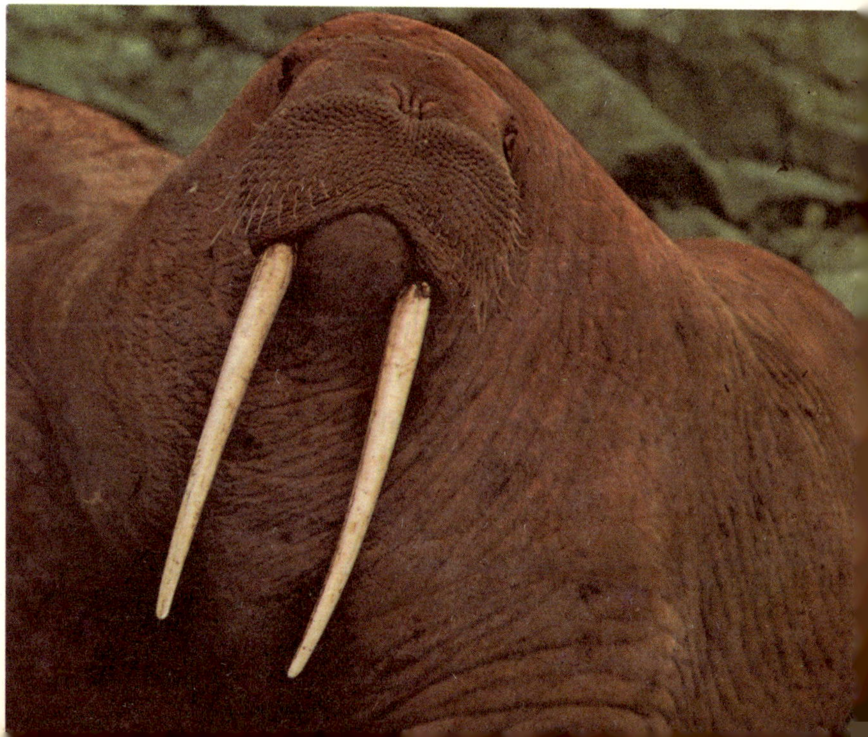

The walrus uses his long tusks for gathering food. With them he rakes clams from the mud and scrapes mussels and snails from the rocks. His huge appetite leaves his body covered in a layer of fat that keeps him warm in the icy waters.

gether. A pan of ice is white in the sun, but with walruses it looks black, as though loaded with coal. Those are well-fed walruses in a heap, sometimes fifty or even several hundred of them. They may travel fifty miles on the moving pan while asleep.

Walruses take turns at guarding against a polar bear or a savage killer whale. One head in the pile is always up watching for trouble. When it is tired of looking and grows sleepy, down goes the head, striking the next walrus. There's a grunt and another head comes up to look around. When this head goes down, it strikes another with its tusks. The movement of one disturbs the next, which grunts, looks, and lies down. So, the word is passed around and each takes its turn as sentinel.

When anything suspicious turns up, the walrus on guard climbs over the bodies of those around him and slides off into the water. This stirs up all the others and off they slide. Each weighs a ton or more, and the slithery, squashy mass movement into the water may tip over the pan. When it upends, it dumps the pile of giants into the sea with a big splash.

Sensing danger—perhaps a polar bear—a walrus lookout has crawled over the bodies of the sleeping herd and wallowed into the sea. Now the others awake and make ready to follow him.

THE PRIBILOF MONSTERS

The loneliest place in the world, so desolate and so remote that it is almost unreal, is a group of islands on the fringes of the arctic. These islands are hidden behind storm-battered reefs shrouded in fog, and chilled by gales laden with snow and sleet. They are the tops of ancient volcanoes thrust up in the middle of the Bering Sea. Two of them, about thirty miles apart , are called St. Paul and St. George—attractive names for fragments of the earth's crust that took the men who deliberately sought them twenty-one years to find!

Captain Pribilof, master of a Russian sloop, whose name this group of islands bears, must have passed near the islands unknowingly many times. Finally, in the summer of 1786, in a fog so thick he couldn't see the length of his ship, his old sloop ran against the cliffs. Suddenly he heard "sweet music" coming through the fog from a mile or so distant, and he knew that the search was over.

The "music" was not like the singing of sirens but it sounded just as mythical. It could have been taken for a riot among millions of animals fighting to their death and having a picnic at the same time. They roared, barked, snarled, whistled, wailed, and chuckled, and mixed in

A bull fur seal commands his harem at the arctic breeding grounds, to which the herd of seals returns on schedule year after year.

A female polar bear creeps up on the herd of seals, hoping to catch an unwary pup and make a kill.

Polar bear cubs, like most young animals, are not required to hunt their own supper. They can romp and play, unconcerned, while mother bear goes hunting for seal.

with this unexpected medley was a weird *choo-choo-choo*, like a steam engine starting. This clamor, which came from the breeding grounds of the great Alaskan fur seal, shattered the deep silence of the arctic.

Fur seals seem to consider the Pribilofs the ideal breeding spot in all the world, and maybe it is. Between the cliffs are miles of shelving, smooth rocks, not too steep, which feel good for a moist squashy body to slide over. The climate is ideal also, because during the summer nine days out of ten are foggy and rainy. That keeps fur wet and makes for privacy. Because of the furious gales, even blood-sucking mosquitoes and black flies shun the place. Moreover, the islands are a hundred miles below the edge of the permanent ice floe at its farthest extent in winter, so they are not often visited by polar bears hunting baby seals. Wolverines, weasels, and brown bears do not trespass from the mainland. The offshore reefs keep out the killer whales, so young seals can have safe water for swimming lessons.

No animal ever chose more wisely, or found a better place to serve as a breeding grounds through thousands of years. How the seal found this eerie hideout and first took title to it, no one knows. This probably happened when the reefs and beaches first emerged from under the retreating Ice Age glacier.

The fur seals share ownership only with the birds, which breed by the millions up in the crevices and chinks of the volcanic rock. Seals are fish eaters, and they do not molest bird eggs. On their part, the little auks, murres, and puffins do not bother with the big brutes on the rocks by the shore, but become the audience of the bull fights and the swimming lessons of the young seals.

Although whales and walrus babies take to the sea as soon as they are born, seals have kept more of the instincts of their land ancestors. Seal babies are all equipped with flippers but they have to learn how to use them, how to breathe for long submersion, and how to catch

After the polar bears have eaten their fill, an arctic fox moves in to finish the carcass of the seal.

live fish. They must have a couple of months of lessons before they can go to sea on their own.

Mother seal, very patient, goes through the motions of the lessons in clear water where the young ones can see her. A whale swims by using its tail as a propeller, but a seal moves through the water with powerful strokes of its front flippers. The hind flippers float to the rear and are used as a steering sweep or rudder. A hind flipper strongly resembles a human foot, drawn out to about twenty-one inches in a full-grown seal, with flat instep and usually five toes.

For eight months every year the Pribilof herd of three million seals is scattered through the North Pacific. Since the children born on the Pribilofs during the summer are too young to stand the cold northern waters in winter, they and their mothers swim three thousand miles south, arriving in December to spend the winter far off the coast of mid-California. The tough old bulls, which don't mind the cold stormy waters of the North Pacific, travel only a few hundred miles down from the Aleutians, sleeping on the sea, riding the Pacific currents, catching tons of herring.

In the spring the mysterious call of the arctic is felt by these animals, scattered far and wide across the Pacific. Wherever they are, they all head north with one accord. The assembling of millions of these creatures year after year, for centuries, always on schedule, is one of the great mysteries and wonders of life.

Swimming on his back with his webbed hind feet, the sea otter leisurely consumes a freshly caught crab.

What is the nature of the summons? How can the animals know exactly where they must go? What guides them on their weeks-long voyages to pinpoint locations in the vast north, to the channels through the Aleutian chain which lead directly to their fog-bound rendezvous? How do they navigate such a course of several thousand miles through gales and fog, always arriving at the right spot at the right time?

Snug on a floating ice pan, this ringed seal pup lies close to its mother.

A herd of fur seals at their breeding grounds, on the Pribilof Islands, in the Bering Sea.

The bulls are scheduled to arrive first. A few begin turning up early in May. They survey the coast from offshore for a week or so, and then climb out onto the rocks. Hundreds of heavy bodies roll through the surf and lift themselves onto the land. They have returned to the same locations where they were the year before, but not always to the same rocks.

The bulls are swollen with much feeding. Their necks, chests, and shoulders, two-thirds of their total weight, are enormous. The biggest and strongest are the beachmasters, the bosses. They look around, and each stakes out his claim for a space on the rocks about seventy-five feet long and one hundred feet deep. This is the territory where he intends to keep a harem. From the moment a bull has laid claim to his plot of ground, he rules according to the laws of the jungle. With all his great brute strength, he will defend it in bloody battle.

From the 12th to the 14th of June the females arrive, and in the midst of a great hubbub, roaring, snapping, and fighting, they slide into places in the various harems of the big bulls.

A surplus of young males, called bachelors, is climbing ashore during all this excitement. They are neither strong enough nor experienced enough to set up their own harems. The big old bulls are in full charge of that and, besides, there is no more room available on the seashore rocks. So the bachelors slither through the crowd and take their places higher up on rocks away from the water, where they sit day after day looking over the situation and waiting their turn, which comes when they are about seven or eight years old. Whenever these lonely bachelors want to reach the sea for swimming and fishing, they must use a single narrow path which is allotted to them, and which passes through the harems.

GROWING UP

When one of the bachelors feels that he has grown big and strong enough to command a harem of his own, he leaves the narrow path, barges into the crowd, and challenges a beachmaster. This promptly brings on a terrible battle between heavyweights. Giant bodies writhe and swell with rage. The stored up energy of those huge necks and shoulders fires the enormous muscles. The hoarse roars of the monsters, intermingled with shrill whistles of pain and raw terror, echo from the hills. Hair flies. Blood streams down.

The animals fight until one is so badly torn that he cannot keep up the battle. If the beachmaster in charge before the battle started is the victor, he has won the right to his harem. However, if he loses, the others drive him to the rear, to sit in loneliness and disgrace among the bachelors. He must stay in the background until he dies, which will probably not be a long time away. He is beaten in battle and finished. A new beachmaster has taken his place and assumed all the rights and responsibilities of the harem.

Soon after the arrival of the fur seals on the Pribilofs in June, the seal cows give birth to the year's crop of puppies. These are black and tiny, only eight to ten pounds each—small for animals that will grow so large. In a couple of months they will be fighting each other in imitation of their giant fathers.

During this first summer the babies grow fast while feeding on their mothers' milk and on the fish caught for them. This is their best chance to enjoy being land animals. They gallop to patches of flowers, sleep in the sedge, or roll in the saxifrage.

The big bull fur seal arrives at the Pribilof breeding grounds a few weeks ahead of his harem of cow seals. They mate early in June.

Compared to the noisy bulls, the cows are almost silent. Occasionally they snarl and fight a bit, and after the babies are born their mothers talk to them with a hollow, prolonged baaing. The pups reply with a little bleat, like a lamb's.

The father pays no attention to his family. In fact, mother and child have to be on the alert to move out of the way when the big bull wants to lie down and go to sleep, or the little fellow will get crushed.

The beachmaster holds the fort for perhaps six weeks. Always on the alert for trouble, always ready for a fight, he does not swim, and he has nothing to eat during that time. When summer ends, he is a mere shadow of his former self. He has been living and fighting on the fat energy stored in his big bull neck and in his mighty chest and shoulders. A thin, battle-scarred, and hungry bull at last slips into the water when the harem breaks up.

At about the same time, millions of other fur seals—big bulls, slender mothers, little youngsters—slide away and scatter. St. Paul and St. George are now deserted—just desolate rocks chilled by icy sleet, shrouded in mist. It is not easy to believe that this lonely place was so recently the home of noisy millions.

But it is only a chapter that has come to an end. Come next June, the story will resume. The seals will be back on schedule, as they have been through the ages.

The polar bear swims out to climb up on floating ice pans when hunger sends him hunting for seals.

The spruce and fir trees that mark the northern tree line of our hemisphere face a vast bog which stretches on and on over the horizon until it meets the glaciers and granite mountains of the polar region. This bog is the tundra. Here the ground is permanently frozen, but in summer the top few inches thaw out to form endless expanses of ponds, among which mossy swamps and thickets of crowberry and blueberry bushes develop. Here, when sunlight sweeps the tundra, bringing the spring thaw, all at once a bleak land is converted into the biggest flower garden in the world.

There is no roar or rush of water, no cracking and grinding of ice, as in other parts of the arctic. But of activity there is plenty. The tundra becomes a tremendous mixing bowl of excited life. There are visitors not only from the border areas, north and south, but also from the skies, where an endless number of birds are rushing in, honking and squawking, after curving over half the world to get there.

This multitude of visitors among the wealth of flowers and berries of this wide, weird land, catching the long days of sunlight, shows the sweep of life, and how living things depend on each other. The musk ox comes down onto the tundra from his polar mountainsides; the caribou emerges from his protected winter haunts in the edges of the forest; and the wolverine, ermine, and brown bear also come out of the forest to run on the fringes of the tundra.

During the past winter the tundra was swept by blizzards. Snow poured across it, piling up immense dunes. In the dim light this land looked like the surface of a planet where life has not yet been created. Then during a clear night between storms, when time seemed to be holding its breath, the light of a full moon showed something moving into the tundra from the sea coast.

The white fox traveled during the winter on the ice pack, sleeping most of the time in crevices where ice was broken and piled up by pressure. When the white fox got hungry, it woke up and feasted on the remains of a carcass of seal left by a polar bear. The restless polar bear usually leaves half of its catch uneaten. Lucky is the white fox who finds itself on an ice floe with a polar bear. The bear has a keen sense of smell but poor eyesight, and the fox has no trouble keeping out of sight, downwind. He comes out only to clean up the dishes after the king of the polar seas has had his fill. Thus these two, the big white one never suspecting the presence of the little white one, travel slowly southward on the ice pans.

This young seal, learning to swim in the icy waters, has ventured too far from his parents' protection.

Suddenly the polar bear pounces, stuns the seal with a sudden swipe of his paw, and pulls in his prey.

The large black birds, sitting on nests raised high off the marshy tundra, are cormorants. Overhead fly a flock of ring-billed gulls.

In their need for warmth and food, saxifrage plants and grasses grow close to boulders. These arctic plants have no soil whatever to grow in, but send roots into cracks between boulders to tap the mineral-rich waters the melting glacier leaves behind.

In February, the white fox leaves the pan and heads inland. A curious thing has happened to it. The tip of its tail has turned dark brown. Until now it has been all white except for three black spots—its two eyes and nose. Later it will turn all brown, so that it can hide among the bushes and the mosses of the tundra.

The brown tip of the tail is the first sign that the tundra is going to wake. In some mysterious way it seems to give the fox new energy. He sleeps less and lopes for miles across the snow with his nose down. The deeper into the tundra he gets, the more excited he becomes. He pauses in front of an extra-deep snowdrift with paw uplifted, like a pointer dog. His nostrils quiver as he tests the scent from the hollows, where branches of bushes are sticking through the snow. Then, with a little quick whine, his head goes down under the drift, and snow flies out from his fast-moving paws.

THE LEMMING

The target of the little white fox's efforts is the lemming, whose cities lie deep under the snow. Other animals, too big to find shelter when the thermometer is fifty below, take to the woods south of the tundra. But the lemming is the tundra's permanent winter resident. There it remains after other animals have been driven away by the bitter cold.

This is a friendly little animal you could hold in your hand. Although he looks like a flat, fluffy field mouse, he is rounder and fatter. Fur covers his ears and the tail is so short it hardly shows. A lemming looks about five inches long, and fat, with tiny head and small bones under its fluffy fur. It can glide easily through a one-inch hole. When the snow comes, it can vanish deep underneath that wonderful white insulating blanket. It lives among sap-filled twigs and sphagnum mosses, whose cells are like fresh springs of water. They do not freeze, because they are packed in the warmth of decaying vegetable matter.

The lemming has no need to come up into the air while the snow is on the ground. No matter how bitter the cold above, it is mild down there under the snow, among the twigs and dried leaves. The lemming runs in tunnels that extend for long distances. It rests in cubby-holes anywhere. There is always plenty of bark and dried berries in the labyrinths. Passages lead in all directions, and are exciting to explore.

The lemming eats no meat except an occasional dinner of minute insects and larvae that dwell among the grasses and roots. There is also a wealth of roots, seeds, leaves, frozen berries, and bark, and the lemming eats them all. For clipping and gnawing plants it has teeth like a buzz saw's.

To be healthy, to find food and a mate, and to seek company, the lemming must be able to run around. It has four mouse feet, and claws that can tunnel through soil or debris like a power drill. The network of tunnels, totaling thousands of miles, indicates that this little animal is the fastest snow-removal machine on earth.

The arctic fox is brown until snow begins to pile up on the tundra. Then his coat becomes lighter, blending into the landscape. Not only hunted animals, but hunters too, benefit by such color changes.

Caribou are a type of arctic deer with short tails, shaggy fur, and towering antlers. Herds of caribou are sometimes tended by Eskimos.

Swimming through loose snow is different from digging through packed soil. Accordingly, during summer, when there is no snow, the lemming is equipped with long sharp claws on the two middle toes of its front feet. These enable it to dig around roots. When the ground freezes and the snow comes, the claws begin to grow wider and, instead of being sharp, they are now flat and double the summer size. They have turned into snow shovels!

On the level tundra, masses of live roots, dead leaves, and clumps of sphagnum moss, growing in wet soil, alternately freeze and thaw year after year until they become loosened and lifted up above the permanently frozen ground. In this way a lot of edible vegetable matter turns into a hummock full of nooks and crannies and passageways, like a sponge. With some easy remodeling, these domes will hold any number of ball-shaped nests about five inches in diameter.

The lemmings' nests are lined with grass and saxifrage flowers. The more luxurious are lined with the fur of fox, caribou, or musk ox which the lemmings found on bushes or on carcasses before the snow came. The air in the tunnels is still, and the homes are doubly insulated by snow and by grass, leaves, and hair, and warmed by energetic bodies. Let the winds howl and the temperature drop to fifty below—it's a long way off, above the four or five feet of snow.

A far-flung system of winding, many-branched tunnels runs under the snow between the hummocks. There may be a connected pattern of tunnels running hundreds of miles over the horizon. But lemmings who are raising families do not roam far from home. Each has its own nest and, if it scampers around among neighboring hummocks, it finds its way back home by its own odor. When one lemming

The huge timber wolf has killed a caribou that was too old to keep up with the herd. Wolves have been known to trail their victims for more than 100 miles.

After this pair of timber wolves has singled out a caribou, they will continue tracking it for hours, exhausting their victim, and rushing in for the kill.

passes another in a tunnel, they stop to touch noses.

In the comfortable, secure, well-fed cities under the snow, there is no awareness of numbers—of the millions and millions and millions of lemmings, of how the population is mounting across the tundra. And then one year something terrible happens.

THE DEATH MARCH

In winter, the tundra is still a vista of motionless space, and it gives no outward warning of the approaching catastrophe. Beneath the snow, individual lemmings still touch noses when they meet. Now and then one grows curious about the strange world above the snow and runs a tunnel upward. At the top he blinks at the strange, cold world, then slips back down his tunnel fast—back to the nice warm nest in the roots of the crowberry bush.

By March the lemmings are not meeting singly and touching noses. Now perhaps ten or a dozen are meeting at a time, and they crowd past each other with angry squeaks and nips. When they go visiting in nearby hummocks,

The timber wolf drags part of the caribou carcass back to his den for his cubs to feed on. Wolves often make their homes in dens abandoned by other animals.

In summer, the weasel's fur is brown, helping him conceal himself in underbrush and dead leaves as he hunts for mice, birds, snakes, squirrels, and rabbits.

In winter, the weasel's coat turns completely white, making him almost invisible in the snow, except for his black-tipped tail. Then he is known as an ermine. In the arctic, weasels feed on snowshoe rabbits and birds and take heavy toll of the lemming population.

they find crowds of new nests. They must go farther and farther for fresh roots and grass. By April, spring thaws have uncovered hummocks far and wide across the tundra. The lemmings come out and scamper around, chewing the buds on the bushes. They cut grass, gather it into sheaves four inches long, and take it back into their burrows.

Rich brown fur makes a lemming almost invisible among the red shadows thrown by the low sun. The brown coat has another use: it protects the animal's skin from the cold water which is kept away by the air bubbles caught in the fluffy fur. The bubbles also make the lemming buoyant so that it swims and floats easily. Lemmings cross the ponds of the tundra by paddling furiously with their hind legs while steering with their front paws. Ripples make a long series of V's, and there is a trail of seething bubbles from little paddling paws as though from a small outboard motorboat. When a lemming climbs out it shakes itself vigorously like a dog.

Such a pleasant life is the usual thing, but this is the year of trouble. When the lemmings come out from their overcrowded galleries, they see, not wide-open spaces of fresh grass and quiet pools, but other lemmings putting out their heads from thousands of other holes. Groups are already out and rushing around in circles, splashing in the ponds, dancing in a sort of frenzy, snarling and fighting. There are too many lemmings and the future is beginning to look hopeless for this animal community.

As more and more lemmings pour up from their homes and tunnels, they become panic-stricken. They run around, eat less, and exhaustedly fall asleep in the open—not in the safety of their homes. But a lemming asleep in the open, curled up like a baby porcupine, is doomed. Suddenly, there is the shadow of huge wings, and the snowy owl with outspread claws strikes like lightning.

The panic of the lemmings spreads across hundreds of miles of tundra. It is felt in the polar region to the north, and along the coast where the ice floes are breaking up. It reaches the dark spruce forests to the south. All the life of the arctic surrounding the tundra is set in motion.

Not one fox, but thousands, appear from mysterious hideouts. These have lost their beautiful white coats and are mostly brown, with a few white patches—like the brown tundra moss mottled with patches of snow. Wolves that have been stealthily stalking the caribou, now stand on the tops of hills, heads upraised, sniffing the air, moved by an irresistible call from the tundra.

Out of the forest bordering the tundra, otters, martens, and ermines come running. Brown bears turn over stones on the tundra, looking for panic-stricken balls of bright brown fur. The polar bear climbs ashore to try a diet different from seal.

The frenzied lemmings are forming squads – regiments—armies. They pay no attention to the rapidly increasing raids of the animals with queer squinting eyes and soft paws. They ignore the fast-moving shadows and fierce talons from above.

An older male lemming rushes out of its hole with a shrill squeak and sets off as though it knows exactly where it is headed. Others nearby stop milling around and follow. The leader keeps well out in front, with a dozen or so lemmings at its heels. Back of this advance party come scattered bands of twenty or thirty. Maddened by the crowding in their underground homes and on the tundra, they now press tightly together and surrender all their accustomed little ways of life. Their only urge is to press on.

The rippling brown patches move in the same direction. Millions and millions of little feet patter on and on for countless miles. The armies flow together, growing larger as more lemmings pour out of the tunnels.

The other hungry armies are closing in by land and air. Their raids are multiplying, but the lemmings do not retreat under ground. They only squeak and snap helplessly at the huge beasts that fall on them; the most furious fight that a lemming can make has little effect against its attackers.

Northern animals—like this arctic fox cub—can keep warm by ruffing up their fur, and trapping their own body heat in an insulating jacket of warm air, even when lying on a snowdrift.

The snowy arctic owl swoops down on many small furry animals. He is especially fond of rodents, and his northern visit never fails to coincide with the lemmings' panic-stricken migration across the tundra.

Safe from the cold and fury of the arctic blizzard, the female lemming places her young in a warm, grass- and fur-lined nest deep under the ground.

When the tundra becomes too crowded with lemmings, hordes of little animals begin jostling and running, in panic, to the sea.

On and on the lemmings go, traveling by night at first, and curling up to sleep by day. But as this appalling river of fur flows on the lemmings grow more excited. Now, instead of taking time out to eat and let laggards catch up, they press on, not even stopping to rest by day. A few mouthfuls at most are grabbed on the run.

Often the march ends before the sea is reached—because there are no more marchers. The foxes and snowy owls, the weasels and wolves—that forgot each other to get a share of the gluttonous feast—have appeased their great appetites.

But sometimes millions of lemmings do win the sea. Without hesitation they plunge through the surf, or, if they find themselves on a cliff overlooking the sea, they dive off. The bubbles in their fur make them buoyant, and the cool water feels good. They swim on and on, perhaps for miles. Bubbles foam out behind. But these bubbles are not entirely from paddling feet; the fur of the lemmings is losing its buoyancy.

The big cities on the tundra will be deserted now.

BIRDS OF THE POLAR NORTH

Hard on the heels of spring, the sky fills with the whir of wings, and the polar valleys echo with the honking and squawking of millions of new arrivals. For a few weeks the ragged old musk oxen, the white foxes and hares, and the tragic little lemmings will share their savage and beautiful land with the birds who own the world.

The birds heard the call of the north in faraway places. They heard it in their homes in New Jersey, Virginia, North Carolina, California, and around the Gulf of Mexico. Below the Equator they heard it—in the Amazon Valley, the pampas of Argentina, the Falkland Islands, Tierra del Fuego, and at the very bot-

Before they reach the shore, many fall prey to hungry animals and birds. This lemming has been bitten at the base of the skull and killed by a weasel.

tom of the world in Antarctica. They heard it in Gibraltar, Italy, the Azores, the Canary Islands, and Algeria. The call was heard far at sea in the Humboldt Current off the shores of Peru and Chile, and in the Guinea Current along the coast of West Africa, and in Borneo, the Moluccas, and the Arabian Sea.

Birds living in all corners of the world suddenly felt far from home. They belonged to the granite, glaciers, and tundra of Alaska, and around the Arctic Ocean. Wherever they were, unaware of others doing the same thing, they responded to the call and took to the skyways that lead to the north.

What signal did they receive? How could all act in the same way at the same time? They abandoned homes and food and familiar surroundings as though a trumpet had sounded, and set out to cross open sea and continents—thousands of miles—without hesitation. They headed for the same spot where they had spent the previous summer; they traveled the same course their kind have followed for hundreds of years. They broke through walls of dense fog to fly toward their goal. They arrived on time regardless of the weather encountered on the way.

All other animals of the earth spend their winters at or near home. The Olympic elk lives on the Olympic Peninsula; the buffalo's home place is the prairie; a beaver winters in the home pond; every elephant holds its territory in the jungle, and every lion its territory on the high steppes; many birds—including sparrow, blue jay, meadow lark, and bobwhite quail—never get more than ten miles from their nests.

But everywhere on the ledges of the arctic, beside the boulders of polar beaches, in patches of saxifrage in sun-catching hollows out of the wind—everywhere right up to the ice floes and pressure ridges of the polar sea are nested the birds whose territory is the whole round world.

This ptarmigan has moulted nearly all of his reddish-brown summer plumage. When winter comes, he will be entirely white, matching his surroundings.

When hidden against a background of ice and snow, these white-furred polar bear cubs will not be easily seen—not even by hungry timber wolves on the prowl for food.

The snowshoe rabbit's wide, furry paws help him run over the deep snow—serving as snowshoes. His white fur helps him to hide from the arctic owl.

One nest is that of an arctic tern on Cape Columbia, America's farthest north point of land, on the tip of Baffin Island only a few degrees from the North Pole. A couple of chicks are snuggled in the nest, healthy and happy in their fluffy down as they look over the rim, waiting for their mother to come back with something to eat. A pile of new-fallen snow surrounds them, but when the mother or father returns, it will soon be scooped out. To the family, this is not alarming; they feel perfectly at home.

This nest in the farthest north is utterly hidden in an empire of rock and ice. Even in spring the place is buried often in furious blizzards. Yet, surely, easily, and on schedule, the parents of the chicks flew eleven thousand miles from their other home on the Antarctic Continent, close to the South Pole. Storms over half the world did not deter them; the length of the Atlantic and the immensity of four continents did not cause them to lose their way. With no navigating instruments but the organs and nerves in their small bodies, they flew above the Western Hemisphere to the same spot where they had nested a year ago.

For many years the voyage of the arctic tern was one of the greatest mysteries of life on our planet. Were the terns in the far north really the same individuals seen in the far south? The exciting truth was discovered when some birds were caught, tagged, and released so they could fly where they wanted. Each tag had a code telling the date and place where it was fastened to the bird's leg. The tag also asked anybody picking up the bird to report to the United States Fish and Wildlife Service the date and place where it was found.

As time passed, reports of the recovery of a few terns began to come in. More were tagged and there was more patient waiting. Banding started in 1913, and by 1948 enough reports had been received to make clear the story of the tern.

Leaving their birthplace in the ice and pressure ridges that surround the North Pole, the terns head southward around the first of August. They fly over Kane Basin, where many polar expeditions have been destroyed by the ice. The eternal glaciers of Baffin Island can be seen on the right, while those of north Greenland are on the left. The terns follow the coast of Greenland to where the shores of North America fade from sight across Davis Strait. After fifteen hundred miles they reach the southern tip of Greenland, where they turn east to pick up Iceland and then head south again. The Orkneys and the British Isles pass below and the terns pick up the coast of France.

On they fly. A tern on its voyage pauses only briefly to circle over the water with beak pointed down, as though taking aim, and when a fish is spotted near the surface, he closes the V of his tail, snaps his wings tight to his body, and dives straight as an arrow.

When the west coast of Africa comes into sight, the terns follow it to the westernmost bulge, where they have a choice of routes. Some fly westward, picking up the easternmost cape of Brazil, and then continue southward along the coast of South America to Tierra del Fuego and Antarctica. Others may choose to

The blue goose hatches her eggs in a nest built on the ground, in the Canadian tundra. She will spend the winter in Louisiana—about 3,000 miles away.

Lesser snow geese (white with black wingtips) and blue geese, with newly-hatched goslings, at their breeding grounds in the arctic. Their nests are found over a huge area that stretches from Siberia to Baffin Island. Although differently colored, they belong to the same species, and interbreed.

Snow goose goslings explore the marshy tundra in northwestern Canada. They must learn to fly quickly, so that they can practice for the long migration to the south.

This goldeneye duckling will feed on a diet of mussels, crayfish, and insects. Adult goldeneyes are called "whistlers" because of the sound their wings make while flying.

When this peregrine falcon chick is full grown, he will have gray-blue plumage on his head and back, and a barred breast. This bird is usually known as the duck hawk.

follow the coast of Africa all the way to Cape Town—and then head two thousand miles across the South Atlantic to Antarctica.

How do they do it? How can a bird find its way over an exact and specified course—from point to point? Much of it is seeing perhaps, but they travel mostly at night. And what about fogs and the storms that blow them off course? How does a bird recognize the coastline and the landmarks? Who gave it a chart and told it how to use the chart? How does it time a flight that lasts for weeks so as to arrive at the goal on a certain day? If it goes from one visible point to another, how does it steer its course when it is flying a mile or two above the sea?

Many days of the amazing flight of the arctic tern are spent far out of sight of landmarks, crossing oceans as unerringly as though they were lakes. The golden plover, which is not a sea bird and cannot rest on the water, flies the Pacific—over two thousand miles of open ocean—between Alaska and the pinpoint islands of Hawaii. The greater shearwater nests in one tiny place, an island named Tristan da Cunha, which is located in the middle of the South Atlantic. From there, the bird flies to its nest in the distant arctic.

All sorts of explanations have been suggested by people whose curiosity knows no bounds—and any one of them is plausible, because nature is full of miracles. One idea, not respected by many bird experts, is that the long-distance flyers are guided to their spot in the arctic, and then on a certain day back to their spot around the world, by magnetism. Men use magnetic compasses, but these have to be corrected. When man takes his compass far north, he gets above the magnetic pole and his compass points backward. He has to correct it with some complicated mathematical figuring. Nobody knows whether nature gave these birds compasses that are self-correcting!

Birds have a sense by which they correct their direction when they are following the lines of magnetic fields that sweep around the earth. This sense, or instinct, is beyond anything we can imagine. It is not merely a matter of aiming at the Magnetic Pole, as does a compass

This flock of ring-billed gulls has chosen for their nesting grounds an island in one of the Alaskan lakes, where fish and insects are plentiful.

needle; this would not take birds to their goals, which are scattered all over the arctic. The North Magnetic Pole is located just above Hudson's Bay and birds would have to fly north of it, or east and west to reach their nests.

Another suggestion is that the birds can feel the rotation of the earth in their ears just as you can feel the rotation of a merry-go-round. Perhaps this feeling keeps them exactly on course. If birds can steer themselves from hem-

On the Newfoundland coast, amidst a flock of black-backed gulls, is a skua (left foreground). Skuas often steal another bird's freshly caught fish.

isphere to hemisphere by "listening" to the rotation of the earth, they are way ahead of us in guided missile development!

The best explanation is that the birds are guided by light. We know that bees can reach a distant point by steering according to the angle of sunlight. Why not birds, too, on a much bigger scale?

It is sunlight that calls to the birds. This is what they seek in the far north. Their inner mechanisms are quickened by long days. They have the urge to mate and lay eggs. The ultraviolet rays that are strong in the arctic also help them to make more lime for egg shells. So the birds that fly from far corners of the world into the arctic are called by light, and they are reaching for the sun.

Except when the arctic tern passes from the antarctic to the arctic and back again, it experiences very little darkness. Most of its life is spent where the sun never sets. The arctic tern, who lives both at the top and at the bottom of the earth, is thus the only creature in the world that enjoys almost continuous sunlight.

After stealing an egg from the nest of a ring-billed gull, this weasel bites through the shell and begins his feast. Weasels often eat young birds in the nest.

Birds of many kinds fly to their places in the arctic when spring comes. All hear the same summons, all have the same urge—to lay eggs and raise families where the days are long, where there are plenty of fish and seeds to eat, and plenty of room without much danger from natural enemies.

Eiders make the most comfortable nests. They raise chicks safely on an exposed low rock in the midst of the polar ice pack, which is swept by bitter gales that would freeze a big animal or blow it off the rock. All that an eider needs is a small depression out of the wind, and brimful of sunlight. It plucks down from its breast and lines the nest with this fluffiness that lets sunlight filter through but captures its warmth in dead-air pockets. An eider's nest is warmer than the air above. Little chicks, however, don't seem to mind coming out from under their eiderdown quilts.

Eiders are the only birds that cultivate plants. They fertilize a circle in the hollow of a rock, and after a few years a dense growth of grass forms a beautiful living rim for the nest.

Each year the rim grows wider and deeper from the addition of new grass pressed into it. The eiders and their descendants return year after year to the same big nests. These are like old family castles of the eiders, clustered together on rocky islands of the polar region where they remain undisturbed for years.

Murres stow away their eggs on crannies and ledges of the steepest cliffs. No fox could ever climb up there. They do not build real nests but simply push a few stones around so that the eggs will not roll off the bare rocks. They crowd together almost shoulder to shoulder—thousands on the face of one cliff.

A murre does not move, once it has established its breeding spot. It sticks to that square foot of ledge, and the same murre turns up on the same ledge year after year.

The rocks in the vicinity of the murres ring with the hoarse mating call of this bird—ha-ha-ha—ha-ha-ha—over and over again.

Above the murres the little auks, or dovekies, make their nests. Where the murres swarm by the thousands, the dovekies swarm by the tens of thousands. Let a mysterious alarm be sounded —perhaps a school of herring has turned up in the water at the base of the cliff—and dovekies come off the cliff in clouds. Caught in the light of the low arctic sun, they sparkle like snowflakes above the cliffs, blood-red with lichens.

Dovekies are not so light and airy when they plump down onto the water. They bob around heavily, low in the stern. It is quite a job to be airborne when you're so low in the water. A dovekie may have to boil along like a motorboat for a hundred feet or more before it can rise—unless it gets a boost from a wave.

The phalarope is the ballet dancer of the arctic bird community. While father does the baby-sitting, mother swims in circles upon the surface of very shallow waters. This circling looks very pretty and rhythmical, but that is not why the phalarope does it. She is stirring up the bottom to bring little tidbits up nearer the surface, where she can eat them without diving.

The puffin may have arrived on the scene after other birds had laid claim to the cliffs and windy islands. So the puffin digs hollows and raises its family underground. It likes the tundra better than the rocky cliffs, especially along the coast where it faces the sea for fishing. Puffins are related to the auks and murres, but you would never guess it. The puffin's bright colors and oversized triangular beak make him look funny as a clown.

Canada geese go north high in the sky, in a perfect elongated-V formation, while the deep honking resounds afar. The geese travel overland to their places in the tundra.

Jaegers, the hawks of the arctic, head in from the sea, but are silent. The jaeger likes to have terns and gulls do the fishing for him. When it sees one rise, fish in mouth, it swoops down and strikes. The fish falls, and the jaeger dives under and catches its dinner in mid-air.

These are some of the birds who own the whole world—and move into the arctic all with one accord.

The American golden plover builds its nest on the Alaskan and Canadian tundra. The speckled eggs are well camouflaged among the stones and grasses. In the Fall, most of the plovers fly south over Canada, cross the Atlantic, and reach Argentina.

Recently hatched cormorant chicks lie in a nest of sticks, feathers, and seaweed. When they grow stronger, they will feed on fish by thrusting their bills deep down into their parents' open gullets.

Eastward from the Pacific, through the Rockies, stretches the wilderness of the mountain strongholds. Here, on the Olympic peninsula in Washington, a Sitka spruce (center) is outlined against the sea.

The Mountain Stronghold

THE Rocky Mountains rise abruptly from the almost level Central Plains. Their steep slopes, leading up to glaciers and snow, are the eastern rampart of the great mountain stronghold of forests and animals in the Northwest. The opposite rampart of this fabulous area fronts the Pacific Ocean, which is seven hundred fifty miles to the west.

Between these boundaries the mountains contain huge trees, marvelous animals, primitive wilderness. Here are many trees that are totally unlike the familiar ones east of the Mississippi River. Hundreds of years of undisturbed growing have raised the columns of Douglas fir—trees ten feet thick—two hundred feet into the air. Sitka spruce has been drawn from its home in Alaska, as though by a magnet, to join the coastal part of the forest. Red cedar, elsewhere small, here carries its lacy branches up hundreds of feet.

The growth on the Pacific side forms a mysterious rain forest. In the filtered twilight an elk can vanish by simply standing still. A squirrel is almost invisible when it runs up the huge column of a tree trunk. Big ferns curve and stand motionless. Every fallen giant has quickly become a slender green garden of moss and fern, ghostly bright in the misty air.

Westerly winds blowing across the warm water of the Japan Current bring in great loads of moisture. The cool mountain barrier causes these winds to spill much of their water into the rain forest and then, farther eastward, to release the rest as snow on the mountains. This snow becomes locked in hundreds of glaciers which are the sources of streams that carve deep ravines and leap down the mountains in roaring waterfalls. White peaks and black forests stretch from the plains to the Pacific, interrupted by patches of green woods where bigleaf maple, aspen, and alder grow along the quieter waterways in the valley bottoms.

In this virgin wilderness are the hideouts of primeval animals, created by time along with the trees and glaciers. They are the animals of a massive world of big dark forests and ice and rock. These animals, in a fierce, raw land inherited from the mammoths, must be strong and mobile, or peculiarly skilled, to survive.

VERTICAL MAGIC

Here, the mountain tops of snow, rock, and ice are fragments of the arctic that retreated northward long ago. Animals as well as the land prove the comparison. The mountain goat resembles the easy going musk ox that now lives on the shore of the Arctic Ocean. Both animals have a hump filled with fat—reserve energy for the bleak months of winter, when grazing is poor. Both have streamers of wool, blanketing them against below-zero gales that would freeze ordinary animals to death in a few minutes.

The zones of life which follow northward across the face of the earth are, in fact, similar to those which follow one above another on a mountain. In temperate regions, a climber starting at the foot of a mountain travels about three miles north for every ten feet of height. Imagine looking up at a spot only a hundred feet higher along the trail and realizing that it is miles north! The top of the mountain, clearly visible in the sky ten thousand feet up, is the kind of place that might be found three thousand miles north!

This vertical magic is one of the astonishing secrets of the mountain stronghold. The zones are alike—from light-green woods that drop their leaves, to evergreen northern forest, to treeless but flower-strewn tundra, to arctic rock and ice. Zones that run northward across the horizons are, of course, vastly wider than those that run up a mountain.

Huge bears lurk in the shadows of the dense rain forest.

Bare rocky peaks, high above the timber line, are the home of the bighorn and the mountain goat.

Climb to an arctic ledge with the mountain goat. Look down a thousand feet upon a treeless slope strewn with rocks and flat junipers and a wealth of bright glacier lilies, saxifrage, poppies, and gentians. This is the mountain tundra, to which the mountain goat often descends for a good graze. Below that, scattered clumps of small whitebark pine and spruce turn into the compact forest of evergreen spires. Far below the forest, light-green patches can be seen in the lowest valleys, showing faintly through a blue mist. That may be only a few miles away, yet it is an unknown and mysterious world to the animals of the mountain arctic.

THE BIGHORN

Far above the spires of the giant trees, fresh snow on a dangerous ledge shows the prints of cloven hoofs. A bighorn has passed this way, but where did it go?

You have reached the ledge after hours of struggle with clumsy mountain-climbing gear. You can track that bighorn only a few steps. The trail vanishes at the end of the ledge. It is no use to peer over the edge, looking for the smashed body of the bighorn at the foot of the precipice. The animal has chosen to run upward over the face of the cliff, along that narrow cleft. With luck you may catch sight of the big fellow looking down serenely from a pinnacle a few hundred feet overhead.

The bighorn likes it up among the steepest, rockiest crags, where there are snowbanks in the shady spots, and ledges with clumps of arctic flowers. There he can snooze undisturbed in a sun-warmed place out of the wind. With his wonderful eyesight he can pick his routes anywhere, up or down, and go where he will. When he wants to lie down, he paws two or three times and settles himself on the rock. Animals normally paw the ground before lying down to make a little hollow, or perhaps to clear away sticks and stones or small animals that would be uncomfortable to lie on. The bighorn paws bare rock just because that is the right way to lie down.

MOUNTAIN BOUNCING

The bighorn is a mountain bouncer rather than a mountain climber. The sole of each foot has big, soft, elastic pads that spread apart under pressure to make extra-wide contact with the surface of a rock. The shallow, cuplike hoof contains the pads and provides suction to prevent slipping. But the bighorn's feet are also pliant and sensitive, and operated by powerful muscular springs. He can bounce six feet straight up to a ledge, or sixteen feet across a chasm.

In these mountains there are no absolutely smooth and perpendicular cliffs. The steep slopes always have cracks and little ridges and crannies and footholds. Bighorns can go where they want to go.

Once a herd of twenty-five bighorns was cornered where walls of rock rose hundreds of feet straight up. The only exit appeared to be blocked. But the bighorns picked out a fold in the rock and one after another, without a pause, they bounced this way and that up the fold and disappeared over the top. These were

With no scent to betray him, and spotted with the dappled light-and-shade pattern of the forest floor, the fawn can hide by merely standing still.

two-hundred-pound animals, and a second's pause would have sent them crashing on the rocks below.

Among his arctic heights, the bighorn has little to fear from natural enemies. Only the eagle can look down on him, and the eagle is respectful. The ewe, or mother bighorn, is constantly on the alert for the fierce bird that dives out of the blue to snatch a lamb. While father goes off by himself to bounce among the mountains, mother stays with her young.

She teaches the lamb how to run up and down cliffs and cracks, how to bounce across ravines, and how—if the lamb is a male—to butt another male lamb. The little bighorn also is taken to a place safe for falling, and here he practices bouncing. Often the mothers and their lambs slide down slopes, and bounce up again, bucking each other, and learning to hook, jab, and parry.

About the middle of October the bighorns start down to lower pastures. Days of loafing on high mountain ledges, among fresh, delicious flowers, are ending. The mating season is on. Suddenly each bighorn ram is mad at every other bighorn ram. In the open, stony glades between scattered clumps of whitebark pine and alpine larch, terrible collisions are about to take place.

The huge spiral horns of the bighorn grow more curved every year—sometimes turning 360 degrees upon themselves and fully completing the circle.

The mating season of the bighorn begins in late October. Then the mountains and valleys sound and echo with the battles of the rival rams.

THE BATTLE OF THE BIGHORNS

In fighting for a mate, bighorns obey strict rules of combat. They do not slash and tear at each other in blind fury. They take positions, make certain sounds, and follow the procedures by which their ancestors always fought.

The two rivals first stand side by side, facing in opposite directions. They make a few sudden passes at each other, kicking out sidewise and trying vicious uppercuts with their front hoofs. Bighorns are usually silent animals, but now they grunt and snort. Perhaps the sounds are signs of rage, or perhaps each animal is giving the other a last chance to quit.

A bighorn ram charges his adversary, and the two animals smash together head on. They butt, kick, and jab. Sometimes the loser—as in the bottom picture here—is pushed off a cliff, perhaps to his death on the rocks below.

After ten minutes of this, the animals walk about twenty paces in opposite directions. Suddenly they wheel, rear up, run at each other, and crash head on. The heavy, hollow horns resound with a crack that can be heard a mile. Recovering from the shock, the rivals may call the whole thing off and walk away together from the scene of battle, or they may separate again by twenty paces and repeat the crash.

Sometimes bighorns are badly wounded, even killed, by the battering. Jabbing hoofs can cut out deep slivers of flesh. Noses bleed. Horns are splintered and pieces are even broken off, never to grow again. Occasionally a bighorn is pushed over a cliff.

The big, spiraling horns—apparently useful only in the mating battles—are unlike the elegant antlers of the wapiti, which grow fresh every year. The horns keep growing year after year during thirteen or fourteen years of the bighorn's life. Spirals on an old bighorn may more than complete the circle, and may measure four feet in length and fifteen inches in circumference at the base. The dynamic spiral form is used by nature in many growing things, including shells, pine cones, and unwinding ferns.

In summer the bighorn grazes on flowers and grass on the high mountain peaks. In midwinter he retreats to lower forest zones for a few weeks. There he paws the snow like a horse to get at the grass. His emergency rations, if the snow gets too deep, are the buds of aspen, spruce, Douglas fir, willow, and juniper.

Even the greatest bouncers alive find it hard to live in deep snow in the forest. Then Mother takes over. The snow may be above their backs, but she leads her family, single file, with fifteen-foot bounds, the others leaping exactly in her tracks. The children, born last

The mountain goat's fur stays white all year. His eyes are golden yellow; hoofs, horns, and lips are black.

March, are now big enough to keep up. The family, however, will welcome spring, when they can bounce up again to the high ledges.

THE OLD MAN OF THE MOUNTAINS

The bighorn on a far, high ledge, silhouetted against the sky, crowned by huge horns, is every inch an emperor. But he is not the greatest mountaineer. That title is held by the mountain goat, who goes even higher among the glaciers and lives all year above the tree line. Bighorn's colors blend with rocks and pastures, but mountain goat is all white, blending with snow and ice—all white except for his round, solemn yellow eyes and jet-black, daggerlike horns and hoofs.

He seldom hurries except when gaining momentum for a steep climb, or when the pull of gravity makes him hurry down a cliff. He walks deliberately like an old man on stiff legs. When he hooks his hoofs over a ledge and, with long white beard waving in the wind, gazes down at the world of puny animals, he is the Old Man of the Mountains.

Icy blasts, broken crags, treacherous ledges are no bother for the mountain goat. With his hump of reserve energy and his deep, warm fur, he can ignore bitter gales as does the other true arctic animal, the musk ox. The mountain goat has feet equipped like the bighorn's, and he is the most sure-footed animal in the mountains. Instead of bouncing, he climbs like a monkey, the front feet taking hold and pulling up. His three hundred pounds will scoot up steep slippery rock or ice where a man would hardly be able to budge without ropes, axe, and holding pegs; this agile mountain animal can also clear a twelve-foot crevasse with ease.

During winter the Old Man of the Mountains seeks out the most exposed ledges and slopes that are clear of snow, and there grazes on the dead, frozen remains of plants. Any kind of plant materials, no matter how old and dry, can be turned into the muscles of this mountain climber that chews a cud. The first of his four stomachs is a collecting sack, or market basket, which he fills with grass, leaves, and twigs. He can take all day to do this and then find a sunny, windless spot to ruminate—that is, chew over the contents of his market basket. This material wads up into a cud and is pushed into stomach number two, where it is mixed with digestive juices. Then it is raised up to the mouth, chewed, mixed with saliva, and swallowed into stomach number three. After a good kneading there the cud goes into stomach number four, where the plant mash is finally turned into mountain goat.

This easygoing creature has few worries. Occasionally in summer a cougar will slink above the tree line and try to jump him. Then the goat may use the two straight black daggers on its forehead. These weapons, as sharp as meat skewers, may go in to the hilt and send the big cat away screaming with pain.

When spring thaws come, the mountain goat must keep a sharp eye out for avalanches, rock slides, and sudden water. He can usually scramble higher up on the mountains to get above the avalanches and rock slides. Or he

If the cougar can dodge the razor-sharp horns of the mother goat, he may catch a fat kid for supper.

may leap to a safe ledge and give a little grunt as he watches the avalanche roar by.

Of all the wonderful animals of the mountain stronghold, the Old Man remains the most mysterious and the least observed. To disappear he has only to stand still—which he does most of the time anyway. Then he is but a little patch of snow among the rocks.

THE BEAVER

Far below the arctic heights there are quiet streams wandering through woods of aspen and willow. And there are little ponds where an extraordinary animal is hard at work.

The beaver is cutting down trees, building dams and canals, causing a series of events that will affect all neighboring plant and animal life. Frogs and little fishes, water birds, muskrat, mink, and even the giant moose will come where the beaver creates a pond.

The beaver's pond is his fortress, and he could not survive without it. Many wild animals have horns, claws, stingers, kicking feet, or tearing teeth with which to fight for their lives against the sudden death that lurks behind every tree or rock, in every shadow. Some animals can bluff, like a puff adder when it blows out its head and hisses, or a bear when it growls and stands its hair on end. Some animals can take to their heels—darting, scurrying, scampering, running up a tree or disappearing into a hole. But the beaver has none of these resources. Waddling along, lacking the sharp quills that protect the equally fat and slow porcupine, it is easy prey for wolf, coyote, bear, bobcat, cougar, lynx, and wolverine! Its weapons are limited to a fine set of teeth, useful only on smaller animals. It can't scare anything with a snarl. Its legs are capable only of a clumsy gallop. It has no tunnel in the ground, and is slow in climbing a tree. So it has to have the pond. When danger threatens, the beaver can disappear under water and not be seen again. It can dive and live happily out of sight even all winter, without making telltale tracks in the snow—and all the time it is breathing air and living like a land animal.

All depends on the beaver's having a certain depth of water the year around, and plenty of

The mountain goat never leaves his home on the heights of the lofty mountain ranges—not even when they are fast in the grip of winter.

If the beaver cannot find a pond that remains three feet deep all year long, he dams a stream. The dam has a spillway to keep the water level constant.

trees. Aspens are first choice, but red maple, beech, willow, cherry, alder, or birch will do. Such a situation is hard to find. Most ponds get low in dry seasons and are so shallow that they freeze solid in winter; no air-breathing animal can live under the ice. Streams are usually too swift, or they dry up. So the beaver makes a pond that will remain about three feet deep through the dry weeks of summer and the flood time of spring. The beaver makes the situation just right by damming streams that flow among the trees it likes to eat.

TREE FELLING

Beavers are small animals for the job of lumbering. Adults average three feet long and fifteen inches high—around forty pounds.

A beaver can cut down a tree five inches thick in a surprisingly short time. It tackles all sizes of trees. The biggest tree known to have been felled by beavers was a hundred and ten feet tall, with a stump five and a half feet across.

To fell a tree, the beaver stands on its hind legs and grips the bark with the sharp curved nails on its front claws. It spreads its hind feet wide and braces itself with its tail. While the front teeth drive into the wood like a holding fork, the lower teeth cut a deep notch three inches below. Then the beaver tears out the chunk of wood between.

The beaver does not control the direction of the tree's fall by cutting on a certain side. But most trees are on ground sloping toward the water and so they fall in that direction, which

Beaver dams are marvels of animal engineering.

The beaver's four orange front teeth are sharp and strong as chisels. With them he can feed on the smooth green bark of the aspens, or cut down trees for his dam. His forefeet are not webbed, and can be used much like hands to grasp and hold logs, stones and branches, and to plaster chinks in his dam with mud and twigs.

When the tree crashes to the ground, the beaver will trim off the branches and float the log to his pond.

Supplies of branches are weighted down with stones, and sunk at the bottom of the pond for winter food.

Beavers often work together when building their houses, cutting logs and repairing their dams.

is the right way for the beaver. Occasionally the tree falls on the beaver and kills him.

When the cut begins to crackle, the beaver stops, looks, and listens. If the tree doesn't fall, a little more cutting is necessary. When it really starts to go, the beaver freezes. No cry of "timber!" is heard—only a loud cracking in the stump and a swish of branches high in the air. The instant the tree crashes to the ground, all beavers in the neighborhood disappear under water. Then they put their noses out and listen for a while to make sure that no dangerous visitors have come to see what the noise is all about.

DAM BUILDING

A beaver fells a tree for two reasons. He loves to eat the tender bark of the topmost branches. He will use the trunk and larger branches for dam building and repair. The timber is cut into convenient logs, averaging around five feet. The length depends on the distance that the log has to be nudged and dragged to the nearest water. The longer the distance, the shorter the log.

A beaver moves logs to the dam site by floating them there, and if necessary he will build canals to do the job. A beaver pond that has been in use for some years, so that all nearby trees have been cut down, will have canals leading as far as five hundred feet into the surrounding land. A beaver may be almost as busy building canals as he is building dams.

Logs floated to the dam site are green wood that will easily get water-logged. The beaver sinks them into place on the dam by piling on mud and stones. Logs and sticks are laid parallel to the flow of the stream, although often rushing waters push them askew. Stones, twigs, mud, wet leaves, and perhaps the discarded antlers of a deer are thrown on. Before long a beautiful dam has risen, backing up the water deep enough so that beaver can come and go under the ice in winter.

A beaver dam's length depends on the size of the stream. Most dams are not over three hundred feet long. A record dam in Montana was over two-fifths of a mile long.

BEAVER HOUSE

An animal that does not live in a deep hole in the ground or in a hollow tree must have some place where it is safe to raise a family. The beaver has it. His site may be a clump of willows or some large bush surrounded by the water of the pond. To this he hauls brush, sticks, mud, and stones, and piles them on—with an architectural plan in mind. The foundation must be securely made, with extra amounts of stones, mud, and waterlogged sticks. The floor is built on this foundation, a couple of inches above water level. Over this is raised a dome of thatched brush. This is not sealed with mud, like the dam, because the beaver family, which will occupy this house all winter when the pond is frozen, likes fresh air and does not mind a dripping roof.

A secret passageway leads from the floor of the house down into the watery cellar. Having extra-large lungs, beavers can hold their breath fifteen minutes if need be. They can easily come and go under the ice through the passageway without coming into view.

The house is big enough for a man to hide in. John Colter, who discovered the marvels of Yellowstone Park, escaped from death at the hands of the Blackfoot Indians in 1809 by diving into a pond and crawling up inside a beaver house. There he hid until the puzzled Indians went away.

Although the beaver's house keeps him comparatively safe, he sometimes falls prey to a prowling coyote.

A beaver is covered by two coats of hair—coarse guard hairs on the outside and the fine fur that makes up the famous beaver skin. Both these fur coats are oiled. After swimming under water, a beaver gives his fur a good combing with the toe of his left hind leg. This toe, split to form a fine-tooth comb, is used to clean the beaver's covering of fur.

On land the beaver can only waddle about, but his streamlined shape is perfect for speedy underwater travel.

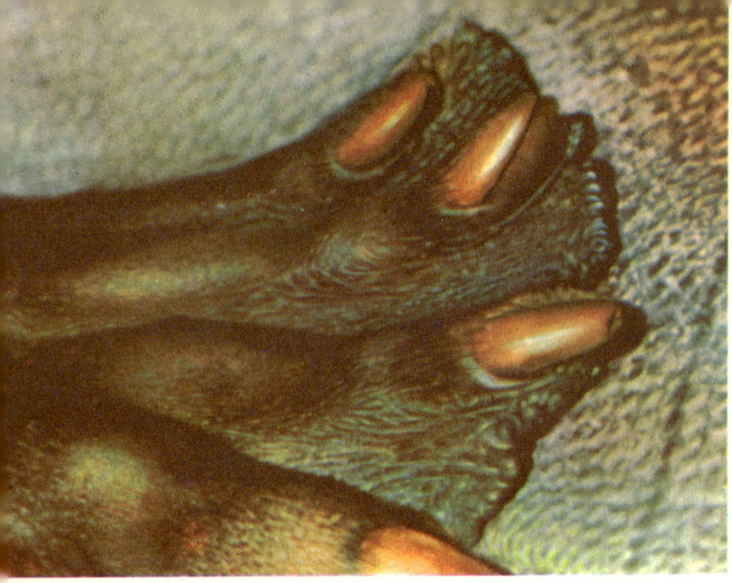

Only the beaver's webbed hind feet are used for swimming; forepaws are folded close to his chest.

Whether lumbering on land or towing logs along a canal or across the pond, the beaver is always alert for an enemy. Sensing trouble, he stops and listens. If the trouble seems real, he slaps his tail on the water, and all beavers hearing this warning sound vanish.

In the depth of the woods, the sounds of crashing trees and the slapping of heavy flat tails are the sounds of beavers. Sometimes the gentle wailing of young beavers can be heard coming from the beaver house. The adults, mostly silent, occasionally speak to each other with low mumbles and whines, sometimes an angry hiss.

Nature gave the beaver unique skills for cutting down trees to build dams and houses. He is the busiest animal in the mountain stronghold, and one of the happiest.

The beaver's tail can be a rudder, an oar, or a danger signal. When he smacks it loudly on the surface of the pond, beavers half a mile away take cover.

THE WAPITI ELKS

Enclosing the green valleys of the beavers and towering over them, the forests of the giant evergreens roll across the mountains. In these forests is the heart of the stronghold. Higher up, winds roar among the crags and drive snow wildly in all directions, but only the spires of the trees quiver when winds hit them. Beneath the spires, the air stirs gently among immovable pillars, and snowflakes filtering down weave a white gauze among the branches. The forest holds a silence so profound that even the sound of water falling a thousand feet over a precipice is muffled.

When the nights are growing longer and the frosts are heavier on the mountain tundra, just at sunset an unearthly sound echoes across the forest. It comes not from the depths within the trees, but from a commanding point overlooking a valley. It starts as a hoarse, guttural roar of tremendous volume, like the safety valve of a big engine suddenly letting go. It rises in pitch with a bugle-like tone, higher and higher, growing more shrill until it soars up to become a screaming whistle; then it breaks and drops, becoming guttural again, and suddenly fades. There is a second of silence, and one loud grunt.

Up in the high pasture, the great American elk, called wapiti by the Shawnee Indians, has challenged all the world to a fight.

More than any other animal of the mountain stronghold, the wapiti reflects the grandeur of the primeval forest. His tall body is carried on long, powerful legs; his shoulders and neck are massive. When, in the fall, he leads the females to a high spot to let the world know he is ready for a fight, he seems to challenge even the great trees. He fills his lungs with an enormous breath of the mountain air, raises his muzzle toward the sky, and pours out his bugle call.

This is the time when the wapiti's royal antlers have reached their full growth. Those antlers are one of the miracles of nature. Growing them, and then finally brandishing them while he bugles, seem to be the whole purpose of the wapiti's existence.

In winter, the beaver is kept warm by the pad of fat he has stored up, and by his glossy pelt. Still later, when the weather gets colder and the surface of his pond is covered with a thick sheet of ice, the beaver can no longer leave his house in search of food. Then he must stay inside, feeding on the branches he sank to the bottom of his pond during the summer.

In the fall, when ice begins forming on the edge of the pond, the beaver family retreats to its island home, safe from bitter weather and hungry enemies.

Every year at the end of winter the antlers break off from a knob that sticks up an inch above the skull. Both antlers fall off at about the same time. The knobs get fuzzy, and two weeks later they have swelled up several inches higher. Antler growing continues rapidly; in a month they are a foot high. The thick velvet is filled with blood vessels that put down the bone which will become the antlers. In about four months, they will be the most magnificent antlers of the animal kingdom.

The main stem, called the beam, turns back over the elk's head and one day, at the right time and place, two spikes come out on each beam. They point forward over the elk's brow and then turn up at the ends like a cowcatcher. Meanwhile the beams sweep backward and then upward, branching and rebranching until the full-grown antlers stand as high as four feet above his head.

By late summer the antlers are finished, the blood stops flowing around them, the velvet dries. The wapiti, who seems in a hurry to have his antlers polished and neat, plunges them into bushes, pawing the ground and shaking his head up and down until all the velvet is scraped off. In September, he is ready for a duel.

THE DUEL OF THE WAPITI ELKS

The place is a high meadow surrounded by clumps of evergreens, with mats of juniper underfoot and rocks strewn here and there. Our bugler seems to be waiting for something. He is standing apart from the harem of a dozen wapiti cows, who are grazing indifferently.

With the beaver safe in their winter stronghold, the coyote must scour the woods for other game.

The wolverine climbs trees hunting for bird's eggs. This ravenous hunter also eats young birds out of the nest. He is the largest member of the weasel family.

Presently a few more cows turn up, and the herd is joined by some other males with tall new antlers.

It is high time.

The challenger bugles again. Another male utters a harsh bark that sounds like "Enough!" He steps out of the shadows of the trees and walks slowly toward the challenger.

The manes on the two animals rise. Their big necks throb. They put their heads down and advance upon each other. Antlers meet and creak like branches of trees scraping together in the wind. Each warrior spreads his feet and gives a couple of powerful pushes.

No reckless charge, no crash of antlers, upsets their royal dignity. If one elk feels the other has the greater strength, without more ado he walks off the field of battle. The victor takes the harem, while the loser goes off alone, perhaps to ponder that he is getting old.

But if they are evenly matched, they will keep on pushing and twisting and grunting. Once in a while they pull apart and glare at each other with an angry snort, and back off about thirty paces to come together again. One may get a bloody nose and some gashes.

Sometimes the pushing contest goes on for twenty minutes or so. The rivals are so busy that they do not notice their audience walking out on them. The males who held back when one of their number accepted the challenge divide up the harem, and everybody leaves.

The pushing contest, however, may have a tragic ending. Antlers of wapiti elks are not just bumpers. They are tough and springy, and they have complicated branches which do not exactly meet. As they are pushed together and twisted this way and that, they may become hopelessly locked. Then all the power of the big animals cannot pull them apart. Locked together, they will die of starvation in a few days. Bleached skeletons with antlers intertwined have been seen on the high pastures of the mountain stronghold.

Wapiti are the most dignified occupants of the mountain stronghold. The nose bridge is wide and strong, the eyes big and wise, the throat deep and heavy with hair. And the finest antlers in the world look more like royal symbols than vicious fighting weapons. Wapiti usually stride deliberately on their long legs, though a cougar striking from an overhanging limb will send them sprinting off at thirty-five miles per hour, whistling like an engine coming to a crossing.

THE WAPITI HERD DESCENDS THE MOUNTAIN

All summer the herd has been feeding on the lush flowers and grass of the high mountain tundra. Now, as the nights grow longer, a sudden storm covers the grazing area with four inches of snow.

This is no problem to the long-legged wapiti. They paw the ground like a horse, clearing a spot for good eating. Flowers and grasses here,

The bull elk shed his antlers in January. A new set replaced them in early spring. During the summer they are in the "velvet" stage (as here) and become sharp and hard by fall, at the beginning of the mating season.

like those of the far north, stay fresh right up to the solid freeze of winter. The grasses keep flowering and the flowers keep opening their buds, displaying delicate stamens and pistils as they do only in the springtime down in the green valleys. To the wapiti such plants uncovered under a light snow are cool and fresh and good to munch.

But four inches of snow on the mountain meadow is a signal. By age-long custom, the herd must start south. Day by day, now, they feed lower and lower, while animals come together from across the valleys and the herd grows larger. Perhaps nature has taught them that there is safety in numbers—safety from the cougar and the bear, for example—as the elk travel far from their accustomed haunts. Or perhaps these animals simply enjoy rubbing shoulders when they migrate. Whatever the reason, the harems come together into herds, and little herds join to make big herds, and a big parade fills the downward trail. If a heavy blizzard strikes and piles up several feet of snow, the travelers push on faster, their long legs kicking aside the light, fluffy snow. In the face of snow and enemies they push on, passing through dangerous defiles, crossing angry streams. It is the age-long custom.

At last they reach a low valley, protected from high winds, where the ground is often clear under the bushes and trees. They have gone perhaps thirty-five miles in all—not far as migrating birds measure distance. The distance varies with every herd. However, the vertical distance multiplies the horizontal many times. Taking advantage of the vertical magic of the mountain stronghold, the elk have reached an entirely different kind of country—in the hope of finding good grazing all winter.

The greatest danger to the herd comes when snow covers plants so deeply that they cannot be reached by pawing, or when a hard freeze follows a thaw and the ground is under a coating of ice as hard as steel. Elk are not made to cope with frozen ground and thick ice. Their hoofs are quickly worn; their noses get cut and bloody from trying to reach grass under a heavy crust; their leg muscles, not powered for continuous effort when the snow is five or six feet deep, eventually crumple under them.

Under these conditions the desperate herd turns from grazing to browsing—eating twigs

The timber wolf stalks the elk herd in winter, waiting for calves to stray away from their mothers, or for an old elk to tire and lag behind the main group.

and buds on the evergreen trees and aspens as high as they can reach. Such things are sticky and bitter compared to green leaves; they are emergency rations at best.

As the lower branches of the forest dwindle, these animals which started their march down the mountains big and strong, with a good supply of reserve fat in their swollen necks, get thinner and thinner. Cougars gather in the dark forest, waiting for low-cost dinners on carcasses of exhausted, starved animals that have dropped in their tracks. The fine wapiti herd is close to calamity.

The herd is saved only by the first balmy wind of spring and the thaw that makes the massive snow and cruel ice vanish into thin air. Then antlers fall from the heads of the bulls, and survivors head back up the trail to the high pastures where wapitis are happy.

THE COUGAR

All animals in the mountain stronghold are afraid of the cougar, who lurks everywhere—from plains to tundra. At the slightest hint of this killer's presence, the mountain goat darts up to his highest hideout. The bighorn's kingly crown is useless when the big cat strikes, and the tall wapiti with his beautiful antlers is

When snow lies too thick to be pawed from grass and leaves underfoot, the wapiti elk feeds by browsing on twigs, bark, and evergreen shoots.

All the forest creatures fear the giant cougar, or mountain lion. He can spring 40 feet from the branch of a tree, breaking the neck of his victim.

easily brought crashing to the ground. Down in the valley, a beaver is crushed by the cougar's blow as though struck by a falling tree. Where a herd of mule deer is browsing in an open glade, one is suddenly, without warning, struck on the shoulder by an animal projectile weighing one hundred fifty pounds. The survivors wheel in terror, flashing white patches on their rumps, and making off in every direction.

When mule deer scent a cougar, they race off, bounding high in the air, traveling forty miles an hour.

Only the lazy porcupine and the sober little skunk have tricks ready for the cougar. Porky twitches his tail, and the big cat's nose is a pincushion. After each needle has stabbed deep, a tiny barb juts out, and now the fierce needles cannot be pulled out without tearing the cougar's nose to shreds. He will not be able to eat for a while.

The skunk's trick is not deadly, but it hurts the big cat's pride and spoils his fun.

The cougar glides among the mountains as silently as the shadow of an eagle. He is one of the most beautiful creatures that ever lived. When he prowls, his lithe body elongates and the skin ripples with smooth, muscular power underneath. When he crouches and freezes, just before a spring, his huge paws are gathered under his body, his shoulders expand with bunched muscles. He springs as though shot from a gun, with two long bounds and a short one, onto the back of the victim.

The tail, wonderfully long and sensitive, steers the animal in the air like feathers on a giant arrow. A cougar hits the bull's-eye. When the cat springs on a mule deer, its outspread claws hit the shoulder at a certain angle. The head snaps back, breaking the neck, and the carcass of the deer is tossed twenty feet by the blow.

The cougar is the best athlete among the big animals of the mountains. Only twenty-six inches at the shoulder, he is low enough to scoot under branches and fallen trees—an advantage in a forest obstacle race. His body, all muscle and unburdened with fat, elongates to seven feet. A white-tailed deer is faster in a burst of speed, but a crust on the snow will trap or cut the deer's legs, while the cougar can spread its great paws like snowshoes. The cougar can broad-jump thirty feet from a running start, and forty feet from a rise or from the limb of a tree. He can pour himself off a ledge sixty feet high, landing on his feet and legs which make perfect shock absorbers.

He is stealthy. Twigs rarely snap under him. Leaves do not rustle as he glides past. He does not hiss, grunt, or snort. All his ferocity is pent up in muscles. Occasionally only a mysterious, wailing shriek breaks the silence of the forest from some far-off, high, rocky ledge where the cougar has a cave. This is the voice of the strange and wonderful animal that haunts the mountain stronghold and is the terror of all its inhabitants.

After the mother cougar finishes training her young, they venture off on hunting trips of their own.

Cougar kits are born in spring, and may live two years with their mothers.

Early in winter, still carrying her young, the female black bear hunts a cave that will shelter her from snow and bitter winds.

Sleeping inside her rocky cave, her thick shaggy coat will keep her warm. Her body will feed on the thick layer of fat she has stored up during warm weather.

While wapiti elks are struggling in the deep snow, reaching desperately for bitter twigs and pine needles, black bears are dozing in their dens. They are the most comfortable old animals in the deep forest.

The black bear can eat whatever is handy—flesh, fish, green leaves, fruit, or insects. The male eats and sleeps while the mother feeds and brings up the children. A black bear in the wild forest spends his casual life within five miles of the place he was born.

Even the deadly cougar is not a great worry. Bear meat is a third or fourth choice on his menu. In summertime the cougar is chiefly occupied with deer. The bear, which seldom pursues an animal but stands and waits near a trail, is a genius at turning into a shadow and fooling even the wily cougar.

The black bear comes in various colors that blend with his environment. His coat may be a deep, glossy black, except for a white patch on his chest, copied from a lonely sunbeam filtering through the trees. He may be cinnamon-colored—like an open forest of ponderosa pine, where the bark is made of red plates and the floor is carpeted with red needles. Black bears may also wear fur coats that are brown, yellow, or blue-gray.

In the fall the bear grows steadily fatter. As he eats and eats, the food forms a blanket of fat all over him, until the bear is enormous. At the same time his hair grows longer. In late November, when he gets drowsy, he can lie down and sleep, warm and safe in his four inches of fat and four inches of fur.

The colder the weather, the sleepier the bear. If the male tires of looking for a cave among rocks, or for a hollow in a tree, he may just lie down to sleep in the lee of a fallen trunk or under the dense crown of a tree or in a clump of bushes. But his sleep is not deep, like that of the woodchuck, ground squirrel, or bat. The bear's temperature does not fall, but stays around 98 degrees. Now and then he gives a little grunt, a whine, and a jerk. He may snore loudly—and the next minute, if the air is warm for winter, stand up and shake himself and

Bear cubs climb trees hunting for birds' eggs, insects, nuts, fruits and honey. They will stay with their mother until their second summer, learning all the hunting tricks and woodland ways that their anxious parent can teach them. After that, she will desert them.

perhaps take a walk. Only half asleep, he is ready to scent danger or, if need be, look for another den.

The mother bear's den has been carefully selected. If it is a cave, she will floor it with leaves. If it is an overturned tree giant, she hollows out a den, at the base, where the roots are upended, and lines it with grass, pine needles, leaves, and bark.

Her big warm body almost fills the place. Nothing could be warmer and cozier for the babies when they arrive in January. Usually

While her twin cubs (left) are busy learning how to climb a tree, the mother bear (right) creeps up on a porcupine—a great delicacy. Then she calls her cubs to show them how she flips the little animal over on its back, and eats it without getting her nose full of quills.

Young bear cubs explore hollow tree stumps with eager paws and noses, looking for stores of honey.

twins, but perhaps triplets or quadruplets, they are surprisingly small to be born of a five-hundred-pound mother. They weigh about half a pound and they are blind, toothless, and hairless.

The nest is less than thirty inches across, but big enough to give the cubs room to grow. The new babies grow fast on their mother's rich milk, which her body makes out of the deep fat that surrounds it, while she gets thinner and thinner. All the time, mother hardly wakes up. She has no hunting to do, and the babies don't wander away and get into trouble. They squeal and kick a little, but they too are dozing most of the time.

After six weeks the cubs have grown to four times their weight at birth. Each is a foot long and covered with silky black down. Now the den is getting a bit crowded. But this is according to nature's timetable. Spring is coming over the mountain, and they can all come out and stretch in the open air. At four pounds, each of the little bears stumbles out on wobbly legs to get his first taste of bear food, which is about anything. For their first feast, the mother may root up a nice fresh skunk cabbage.

During their first six months, the cubs trot along close behind the big, rolling rump of their mother. She teaches them how to dig up wild onions, lily bulbs, wild parsnip, sweet flag, and bear grass. She shows them how to recognize the whiff of chipmunks, mice, marmots (called *woodchucks* in some places), and

Squirrels are sometimes tricked by wily cubs—for young bears often climb trees, and shake down all the nuts from the branches, stripping them of the squirrel's favorite food.

Bears are expert fishermen, wading into streams to catch a fine fresh salmon.

ground-squirrels, and the best way to dig them out of their burrows. She stands guard while they develop their muscles in games of tag, somersaults, wrestling, and boxing. When a porcupine drops to the ground from his perch in a tree, the babies learn that a black bear is one of the few animals smart enough to enjoy porcupine meat. He just puts a paw under the slow, stupid porcupine and tips it over. The soft underparts present no trouble such as the cougar encountered.

Often a deep snow descends on the mountain forest in spring. The little family is now too big to go back into the den for protection and, besides, bears are happy-go-lucky and can usually find a way to have some fun. In this case they all decide to take a walk. Mother bear breaks the trail by jumping, making a big deep hole at every leap. The little ones must jump into these holes or get hopelessly buried. When the mother gets well out in front, she sits down and waits patiently for them to catch up, floundering and whimpering. If she were a grizzly she would carry on a conversation with her cubs on walks through the forest, grunting and whining to advise them and urge them on to greater efforts. Being a black bear, she is silent most of the time, teaching by the power of example.

Observers have told us that, when danger is suspected, she says, "*Rough—rough!*" This means, "Stop whatever you are doing!" A single "*Rough!*" means "Get up that tree fast!" Let a little bear delay and it gets a cuffing that it will remember all its life.

Once bears are up the tree, they dare not come down until they hear the grunt from their mother which is the all-clear signal. If she chooses, they may stay there a long time while she goes off to pick berries or have a few hours of freedom from children at her tail.

Once taught by the mother, bears climb trees better than any other big animal. They do no feeding among the limbs, but the sense of security felt when they were very young stays with them and makes them enjoy climbing. A bear of several hundred pounds will sprawl on a slender limb and go to sleep with his legs hanging down on each side.

A good-sized tree makes a good bear bulletin board. When a black bear discovers the lair of an enemy, a lush patch of berries, or a hollow tree with a store of honey—anything that makes news—he may head for a certain tree, usually

Bears like to prowl close to home, usually hunting over a range of 5 or 10 miles. The mother bear is stern with her cubs, and cuffs them when they disobey.

an aspen, which has smooth bark. This tree is known to all bears in the area as a message center. The bear stands on his hind legs and, reaching up as far as possible, sinks ten front claws deeply into the bark.

Bear trails are well-beaten paths. But a man cannot follow them as easily as he can follow wapiti trails, which have plenty of headroom for high antlers. Bear trails run under fallen trees and through low tangles of brush. They lead to and from berry patches or drinking water or places where the fishing is good. Many generations of bears have used them, and no bear would deviate the least bit from the trail which the first one took. Later, a bear might find a shorter cut to take, or it might be easier to go around the end of a fallen tree than to squeeze under it. But wherever the trail leads, that is the way every bear will go.

BEAR SCRATCHING

Like all furry animals, the black bear wears two kinds of hair. The outer coat is coarser and longer, and the inner is fine—fine enough for the bearskin hats of the famous Grenadier Guards in England. The beautiful, shining coat is shed every spring. Ordinarily the best-groomed animal of the forest, the bear seems annoyed when his coat starts to come out and looks ragged. For a few weeks bears do everything they can to hasten the unsightly shedding. They rub and rub, scratch and scratch, against trees—hour after hour, day after day. Bark is rubbed off as well as hair. The bears jump into thick bushes and scratch back and forth and from side to side. This must feel wonderful, and a lot of hair is left behind.

Bears are crafty fishermen. A black bear stretches out on a log and lets his arms hang in the water with paws open. He waits in that position patiently, not moving a muscle. He may even catch up on a little sleep. Finally fishes can't keep away any longer from that big paw, which is nice and greasy. Then—*Splash!*

The bear sits up with a fish squirming in his paw. He bites off the head and lays it carefully on the log beside him while he makes a deli-

In summer, bears have no definite home; they sleep where they like, and when they choose.

cious mouthful of the rest, bones and all. At the end of the day a little mound of fish heads lies on the log.

A mother may leave her cubs sitting on the bank while she wades in and stands stock-still, belly deep in water. When she feels a fish brush against her sides she makes a lightning grab—and the little cubs are handed a treat.

Bears love to eat nuts that are ripe in the fall, and they know the best way to gather them. Just climb the tree and shake the branches vigorously. Then climb down and pick up the nuts.

A beehive in a hollow tree is the most exciting discovery of all. In goes the huge paw, and out it comes dripping with honey. Of course the bees are in a panic when this terrible thing happens to them. The golden honey is their most precious possession. There is nothing to do but call out the suicide troops and attack the bear.

A bee has a stinger with a fishhook prong, so that it cannot be pulled out. One sting and the bee dies. Yet, to protect their hives, bees will go after a monster bear with utter ferocity. Their stingers cannot touch his skin under the deep fur, but they find his nose. The giant roars with pain, but he goes right on licking the honey off his arms. Bees are licked off, too. Everything of the comb and its little bees disappears.

A black bear shuffles off through the tangled underbrush. Seen from the rear, his high round rump bounces and rotates as though separate from the rest of him. Certainly, he *does* look funny. But nevertheless he is the most intelligent, and the most leisurely, of all the great animals in the mountain stronghold.

During their first summer cubs are playful, while mother bear does most of the hunting. But their mother prods them to learn how to find and dig up edible roots, where to find berries and honey, and how to catch mice, chipmunks, woodchucks, and other small burrowing animals.

The vast, treeless prairie stretches unbroken from horizon to horizon.

Prairie Horizons

On the prairie there are few shadows to hide in and almost no trees to climb. Everything above ground is exposed. But nature has created special animals to live and bring up families here. Instead of climbers of rocks and trees, and hiders in shadows, prairie animals are runners and diggers. The vast flat spaces favor super-runners, and the deep soil invites unlimited digging and tunneling, so that an animal can travel underground mile after mile without appearing in the upper world.

The prairie is the wide-open middle of America. It begins where the eastern woods and hills stop. It reaches westward to the base of the Rocky Mountain rampart, north into Canada, and to the Mexican border on the south. The deep soft grassland of southern Wisconsin, Illinois, Missouri, and Iowa; the rich plains of eastern Texas, the wide fertile levels of the Dakotas and Nebraska; and the sunbaked plains of Montana, Wyoming, Colorado, and southwestern Kansas—all these merge to form the vast continuous space over which pronghorns and coyotes run, and under which ground squirrels, gophers, and prairie dogs thrust their tunnels and build their underground cities.

THE BUFFALO

Go back one hundred fifty years.

Here on the face of the prairie a massive mammal moves in thousands. The buffalo, or bison, has short thick legs—he cannot run fast like an antelope. He has heavy cloven hoofs—he cannot dig like a prairie dog. But he has his own special ways. Instead of running away, he runs toward his enemies. No animal can withstand his fearful roar and crushing power. The huge armies of buffaloes raise clouds of dust which can be seen hundreds of miles away.

The first white man to see a buffalo described it as three animals in one. It had a camel's hump; a lion's high flank, tufted tail, and tremendous mane; and the horns, cloven hoofs, and mad attack of a bull. This was nature's greatest animal experiment in America—a monster too heavy to climb, too big to hide, yet able to survive in the wide-open spaces.

The buffalo's strength and terrible looks are concentrated in front. The heavy head seems to sag, but the buffalo is not tired. He is occupied mostly with grazing on grasses and herbs, and chewing his cud. The position of the head is best for that.

The horns are hollow and curved, wide at the base and tapering rapidly, made for tossing. But the buffalo kills only when another animal makes him mad. With a quick motion of his horns, he can pitchfork an enemy—wolf, coyote, or any other offending animal—out of his sight.

The buffalo's wide head is set under a huge mane. Hair dangles over his eyes and cheeks. A full beard waves back and forth below the chin. That is the way a monarch should look, who is unafraid, unhurried, and slow to wrath.

The buffalo is not startled by an unexpected fright as so many other animals are. If he senses something wrong he stops grazing, he stares, his nostrils expand, he sizes up the situation. If the suspicious object stands still, he will turn away and go back to grazing. If it moves toward him, he will put down his head, paw the ground, utter a few rumbles, and drive forward to the toss.

The buffalo, very nearsighted, depends on keen smelling and hearing. He can smell water many miles away. But poor eyesight is a handicap in the charge. He may stop at intervals and cock his head to take another look. Then on he comes again.

A buffalo walking is like a heavy two-legged animal in front with a smaller two-legged animal behind, pushing. The two legs of the front animal swing slowly, carrying most of the weight and doing the steering. The weight shifts between those front legs with each step. When this front animal throws his weight forward onto the front legs, the two legs of the light rear animal lift off the ground. The hind hoofs dig into the ground with backward strokes that push the animal forward.

The buffalo does not paw the ground like a horse, but when he wants to uncover grass under snow or sand, he pushes with his muzzle and roots for it like a pig. Also, he never rears

The great central plains sweep westward from the Mississippi to the foot of the Rockies.

In winter the herd follows the lead buffalo as he breaks a trail through the snowdrifts. Heavy robes protect them from the icy gales that sweep the prairie.

up. When excited, he tips forward with head down while the hind legs throw up clouds of dust and kick high in the air.

LITTLE BIRDS FOLLOW ALONG

While the buffalo grazes, blackbirds trail him. They feast on insects which he stirs up in the grass. Some birds flit onto his backbone, where they sit in a row, snapping at flies and mosquitoes that graze on the buffalo. On cold nights the birds snuggle into the deep fur over the buffalo's neck and warm their toes.

Prairie fires are often started by a bolt of lightning.

These blackbirds of the western prairie are cowbirds. They build no nests of their own, but lay eggs in other birds' nests. They may throw out other eggs to make room for their own. When the cowbird eggs hatch, the babies are raised by the other bird, who doesn't seem to know the difference.

ROLLING TROT

There are times when even a buffalo is in a hurry. When he is thirsty and smells water, or when trying to escape a blizzard, he moves in a rolling trot. He leans to the right while the right front leg takes most of the pounding and the right rear leg does most of the pushing. Then he leans to the left. Half of him is working at full power while the other half rests. So the huge animal can cover miles without tiring.

In fall, blizzards swoop down on the plains, but this great animal was made for cold weather. Under his magnificent robe he takes winter in stride. At night he faces directly into the blizzard, for his massive front has the longest fur. He sits down and lets the snow drift over him. When the gray light comes over the eastern horizon, he shakes off the snow, eats the grasses and herbs from the bare spot where he rested, and rolls southward again.

THE PRAIRIE FIRE

The biggest animal on the prairie recognizes one deadly enemy—the prairie fire. Fire can cut off his watering place and drive him mad with thirst.

In an extra-dry year, scattered fires may surround a herd. Then some old bull starts moving and the others follow. What starts as a few frightened individuals soon becomes a swift river of rippling brown backs—a stampede.

There is nowhere to run but into the wall of fire and smoke. Many plunge and fall, while others hurry over their roasting bodies. Frantic bellowing mingles with the roar of flames. If the stockade of fire is not deep, some survivors emerge on the other side, with hair burned off, some blind, groaning—standing on black ground where wisps of smoke grow instead of grass.

THE BUFFALO GALLOP

A prairie fire calls forth marvelous speed from monsters usually slow to move. The impulse to stampede shoots like an electric current through the herd. A buffalo sitting on its flank, with legs stretched out, utterly relaxed, when it feels this impulse will spring up and spin in a tiny circle and be off like a deer.

The buffalo uses a gallop more than a run. He plunges with head down, vaulting on his front legs while the light hind feet kick up and down. In the flight of full panic the hind feet push back, making the sand fly, then lift and swing forward together, crossing the front legs as with racing dogs.

Buffalo calves are born in April and May. In a day or two they become strong enough to follow the herd.

THE BUFFALO WALLOW

When the fur robe falls off in midsummer and the buffalo stands naked from hump to rump, thousands of mosquitoes alight on this juicy mountain of meat. If the buffalo can find a willow or a few cottonwoods, he will rub and rub, as bears do in the mountains. But the few trees may soon be rubbed down.

A tormented buffalo may mount to the highest knoll and stand with his face in the wind. Or he may go to low grounds and root around with his head until he finds the softest, wettest spot. The feel of mud on his muzzle will delight him and fill him with energy. He will push and

In July and August, during the mating season, buffalo bulls shake the prairie with their duels.

A herd of buffalo invades a prairie-dog town.

sway and pile up the earth. If water filters into the hole, he will take a cooling bath.

A buffalo in a wallow is one of the happiest animals on earth. His huge body rolls from side to side. He rotates, enlarging the pool. He sinks deeper in the mud until only his head and the top of his hump show. He keeps up a low happy rumbling. When at last he climbs out, mud is plastered all over his body. Now he is a hideous monster indeed!

CORKSCREW SEEDS

In July, a buffalo may sit down to chew his cud among speargrasses which are just now releasing their seeds. Each seed bears a corkscrew bristle. When moistened in the night air it uncoils, and in daytime it coils up, boring like a corkscrew through grass and into the ground. But it does not recognize the difference between the ground and the body of a buffalo. Revolving about eight times an hour, it bores through the new wool on the buffalo and finally reaches the skin. Now the buffalo gets the itch worse than from mosquitoes.

THE BIG MIGRATION

In spring, when the dry northern prairie is changing from dingy brown to pale green, a few lonely buffalo appear. Perhaps these are scouts, which send back scent signals from post to post. Or it may be that the herds to the south catch the fragrance of fresh grass. These herds, constantly growing larger, head north, over worn trails made by their ancestors.

The column of march, twenty miles wide and fifty long, flows northward like a great brown river. The animals travel by day and rest by night. Sometimes they break apart and spend a day grazing. They may be in straggling lines, six or eight abreast, or in long lines in single file, each two feet behind the one in front. Then, as though a bugle were blown, each herd will wheel together and lope along for a few hours.

Buffaloes gather at the river to drink and wallow in the mud.

Pronghorn antelopes search the plains with eyes eight times keener than the eyes of man.

Without grunting or confusion, individuals take positions as if sergeants were marshaling them, the youngest up front and the oldest in the rear. Mothers and children take places in the center. Little buffaloes cavorting among the legs of the bigger ones are flashes of golden brown in a dark forest of legs.

When they sit down to rest at night, all muzzles point into the wind, and a few bulls remain on guard, pacing a wide circle. There are wolves beyond, waiting for a chance to pounce on a young buffalo. But the prairie monarchs are ready to toss any wolf on their horns, leaving the carcass for a coyote to dine on.

The buffalo, it seems, owns the prairie. Always, he and his descendants will wander there, noses to the ground, followed by little blackbirds. They will wheel into line to travel north for fresh pastures in the spring. They will move south from the blizzards in the fall. There will always be millions of buffaloes.

But this was one hundred fifty years ago.

The buffalo did not reckon on the white man, his fences, and his guns.

THE PRONGHORN

All around the buffalo herds, pronghorns watched—to see what pastures the giants were occupying, where they were headed, whether they threatened to stampede. Reports flashed across the prairie from pronghorn to pronghorn over an amazing signaling system.

On each rump of a pronghorn, at the rear, there is a patch of fluffy hair like a huge powder puff, called a rosette. When the animal's big round eyes see something suspicious, perhaps miles away, the hairs in the rosettes stand up and the pronghorn starts to run. When another pronghorn sees a pair of white patches flashing like lanterns, he also erects his rosettes and takes off. Quickly the prairie is dotted far and wide with the white flashes.

The pronghorn is attractive prey for a wolf or a coyote. Depending on keen eyes, sensitive nostrils, and tall ears, the pronghorn must see, smell, and hear from one horizon to the next. Also, he can sprint nearly a mile a minute and, over long distances, hold a pace of forty miles per hour.

September is the time for raising a family; then the exciting fall races of the pronghorns are on. The slender little doe streaks through the grass at top speed, followed by the bigger and stronger buck. Perhaps the doe does not want to hold her top speed, for presently she is overtaken.

Pronghorns are forever running. Two may start a race on impulse at any minute. Little pronghorns play enormous games of tag—tearing off in one direction for a quarter of a mile, then in another for half a mile.

Chimney Rock stands stark and lonely against the prairie sky.

A newborn pronghorn has very big eyes and ears and very long legs, all on a thin, trembling little body. For a few hours it can hardly stagger around. When less than two days old, it will be running twenty-five miles per hour.

Pronghorns have no homes, but each herd has its territory. Fawns are often born on top of a rise—a conspicuous place, but safer than the lower slopes, where heavy-footed buffaloes graze. Once in a while the fawn runs with a playmate, but mostly lies on the ground, long ears folded down flat.

The coyote keeps up a constant search for this delicious dinner, and a golden eagle may wheel overhead. But the little brown heap, exactly the color of the prairie floor, is invisible to all except its mother. It has almost no odor, so the sniffing coyote is baffled. Even the eagle, which hunts with its eyes, is usually thwarted.

The mother is a good protector. She returns to nurse the baby, and although she must graze and gather food, she is never out of sight. If an enemy is spotted, she flashes her rosettes and comes back as fast as the wind. Or she may lead the coyote away by prancing slowly in full view, perhaps limping a little, inviting it to chase her.

The coyote knows he cannot catch a pronghorn in a straight race. He can make forty miles per hour in a sprint and twenty-four on a long stretch, but that is not enough. When coyotes want pronghorn to eat, they must figure out some team play. They must make the champion runner take a zigzag course.

Three or four coyotes can take their stations without being seen, because the coyote is just the right size to travel on the prairie invisibly. His twenty inches at the shoulder does not overtop the grass and bushes as he glides swiftly among them. His size is just right, too, for running in arroyos, the dry stream beds which fan out all over the prairie. Many arroyos are shallow, cut down about two feet, with vertical sides. It seems as though arroyos were made to fit coyotes.

When the antelope fluffs up the fur on its white rump patches, the herd knows danger is near.

Coyote 1 creeps up in the open as near as he can, against the wind. He may be within a hundred feet when the pronghorn suddenly sniffs, stares with big curious eyes, and takes off.

Coyote 1 pursues. His object is to keep the pronghorn running, for even a superb animal runner must grow tired sooner or later.

When Coyote 1 tires, Coyote 2 springs from behind a bush and takes up the chase. The pronghorn changes course, slowing momentarily, and then is off again.

In the second mile, the desperate animal begins to tire. Coyote 3 and maybe 4, too, now dash in to join the zigzag chase.

The climax comes suddenly. The tuckered pronghorn slows to just below twenty-four miles per hour—the top speed of a coyote.

From a distance, a cloud of dust is seen rising from the prairie, instead of two flashing white rosettes.

OUTWITTING A PRAIRIE DOG

The prairie dog is perhaps the most fortunate of the group of little diggers which includes rabbits, gophers, mice, and even the burrowing owl. He has the deepest and best system of tunnels, and a good stock of food in his cool storage rooms.

He builds a circular mound, as much as two feet high and four feet in diameter, around the opening of his tunnel. There he sits as a sentinel, constantly turning his head to watch the surrounding world. If he sees a coyote lurking near, he utters a series of squeaky barks and tumbles over backward into his hole. Duly warned, prairie dogs all over the neighborhood tumble into their holes. None has ventured more than a hundred feet from the home mound.

Prairie dogs are always alert. Even those that are feeding do not leave all the watching to the sentinel on the mound. About every eight seconds each prairie dog stops eating, climbs a clump of grass, rears up, and takes a good look.

To catch a prairie dog, the coyote must use teamwork completely different from that of making the pronghorn zigzag to his death.

A coyote stalks the prairie, hunting for antelope.

The trick takes two coyotes and can be worked only when an arroyo leads close to one of the prairie-dog mounds. One coyote parades openly, letting itself be seen. Comes the warning bark and the prairie dogs dive.

The coyote pays no attention; he acts well fed—not interested in prairie dogs.

After a while the prairie dog which is about to be caught peeks out. He sees the coyote just loafing around, a safe sixty feet away. He does not see another coyote sneaking up close to the mound through the arroyo.

The prairie dog gives the all-clear signal and climbs out of the hole.

The trick has worked.

Twin antelope kids are born early in May. In ten days they are able to run as fast as their mother.

Full-grown prairie dogs are not afraid to venture from their burrows when hunting for food.

THE VOICE OF THE DESERT

The coyote is at home on the open range because he is cut to size and keeps his tail down. He is very friendly with other coyotes. When they meet, they touch noses.

The coyote's cousin, the fox, who lives in woody places, holds high his bushy tail, but the coyote must drag his to keep from being seen. When he is running at top speed, however, the gorgeous tail streams out behind, his ears are flattened, and his long sharp muzzle is thrust far out in front. He makes a streamlined pale yellow streak.

An active coyote needs a lot of food, but he prospers because he can eat almost anything. He has the biggest appetite on the prairie—for all kinds of fish, flesh, and fowl, dead or alive. Because he cleans up the prairie, he has been called a health officer and a garbage man.

At the end of the day, a well-fed coyote gives up the role of unseen hunter. He wants everybody to know he is there and proud of it. At sunset he mounts a rise, points his sharp nose straight up, and lets go. He begins with one low bark and a few whines like an orchestra tuning up. The barks and whines grow louder. Suddenly they change to a drawn-out, quavering wail that rises higher and higher, soaring through two octaves—the call of the wild prairie.

For six weeks, prairie dog pups stay safe in their warm underground nest, nursed by their mother.

THE HIDDEN FAMILY

After this blood-curdling outcry, the coyote retires to his den for some sleep. He has picked out a soft place behind a bush and dug a hole about fifteen inches across. The tunnel may be ten to twenty feet long, depending on how lazy he is. It leads to a den that is three feet across.

In late February, the coyote may bring his mate home, and the den becomes a nest for six well-furred puppies with closed eyes. At that time mother takes over, and father goes off to dig himself another den.

For two months father must live alone, but he never forgets his family. He will try to bring them a carcass every day, laying it at the mouth of the den where mother and babies are hiding. There they are safe from eagles and wolves that would love a mouthful of coyote puppy.

At the end of two months father is allowed to come down to his den again and meet the family. The children are getting big, ready to go out and learn to hunt. Judging by the barking and scampering of father and puppies, this is the happiest time in a coyote's life.

Nobody must know where the coyote family lives. Father never goes straight to the mouth of the den. He circles first, and may even hide behind another bush a long way off. When he thinks he is being observed, he goes straight to another den which he has dug for this purpose, and lays the food there. That den is empty, but how is a wolf or owl to know?

When the father has reason to believe the home den is discovered, he works all night digging another hideout. By next morning, the family has moved.

THE MIRACLE DIGGER

A prairie dog's hole goes straight down, as much as sixteen feet, and the owner goes down headfirst. But he doesn't crash at the bottom. The hole at the top is like a funnel, narrowing quickly from about seven inches to four. It is probable that the prairie dog can slow his speed by bunching up to make himself fatter.

He usually stops about three feet down, at a shelf or little room called a guardhouse. Here

Up in the sunlight, a prairie-dog pup finds a tempting variety of seeds, insects and grasses to feed on.

The mother prairie dog, guarding her children, is always alert, ready to bark when danger threatens.

A prairie dog is cornered by a coyote.

he can safely pause and consider. If the danger is great, he can go down deeper for more security. If, however, he was startled by a false alarm, he can quickly get back to his mound.

How can the prairie dog dig such a deep vertical shaft? He attacks the ground with big sharp claws on his front feet, and kicks dirt backward with his hind feet. That does not explain how he gets dirt, often gravel, ten to sixteen feet *up* a four-inch shaft. Does he back up the shaft, pushing the dirt? Does he turn around and push it upward with his head? No one knows the solution to this mystery of the prairie.

All we know is that he does get the dirt and gravel up and arranges it in a circular dike to keep water out of the hole and to make a lookout perch. He tamps down the dirt on the mound with his broad forehead and flat nose. Somehow he doesn't get dirt in his eyes.

From the bottom of the plunge shaft he runs a tunnel slanting slightly upward to keep it dry in case water gathers in the diggings. At the end of the tunnel, ten to twenty-five feet long, he builds a round bedroom nine inches in diameter. This is lined with grass cut in short lengths and shredded wood. He builds another room off the tunnel for a toilet. No other animal on the prairie has such a safe, comfortable and clean home to live in.

When the sun is shining he goes up the shaft and sits on his mound, or eats grasses and bushes, caterpillars, beetles, and grasshoppers. About the only real exercise he gets, besides galloping and diving into his funnel at every alarm, is to leap and hop around after grasshoppers.

This miracle digger never stores up food. He eats all he can lay his sharp teeth on, including roots and bulbs as well as tender leaves and flowers. But let it be cold and windy, or wet and dark, and he stays below without eating or drinking. His body gets water from the sap of plants and the blood of insects. As to food, he can live a long time off his own fat.

The prairie dog as he sits on his mound makes chirring small talk with thousands of friends all around. Prairie dogs like each other's company. They build networks of villages across hun-

At mating time, the male sage grouse inflates his throat sac and fans out his tail. Then he and the other males dance together, courting the females.

The sharp-tailed grouse lives on the plains from eastern Canada to Alaska, and as far south as New Mexico, feeding on nuts, grain, insects, and fruits.

dreds of square miles, each village occupying two or three square miles, with a mound every ten steps.

WORLD'S CHAMPION DIGGER

The pocket gopher is one of the world's champion diggers. This little creature that weighs about one pound can go through the soil like an underground torpedo.

The gopher builds himself a labyrinth that goes far and wide under the prairie, but he can always find his way home. This home is a ball-shaped room about ten inches in diameter, where he dumps grass and leaves to eat while lying in bed.

The tunnels that go everywhere around the bedroom actually go nowhere. Many are used only once. They are made while the animal is collecting grass roots and underground parts of plants. The gopher almost never comes up into the world of the open air, except at night to gather grass, and also when, obedient to instinct, he leaves his home and visits another burrow to find a mate.

One little pocket gopher can dig a vast tunnel system. Spreading his hind feet far apart, he works his forelimbs—which have long sharp claws like sawteeth—faster than the eye can see. Each strong downward stroke cuts the soil down and pushes it back under his stomach. When the accumulation crowds him, his hind feet come into play and send the dirt flying to the rear.

A pocket gopher turns around in his tight-fitting tunnel by pushing his head between his hind legs. With a twist he faces the other way. This somersault is necessary only when digging, for if he is simply traveling through a tunnel he can run forward or backward with ease. For guidance he has a sensitive nose at the forward end and a sensitive tail tip at the rear end; with this equipment he can find his way in either direction.

He builds a storeroom and stuffs it full of food. For this purpose there are two big outside pockets on his cheeks—not merely big cheeks for holding things, but true pockets with outside slits. Working fast with his forelimbs, he stuffs first one pocket and then the other full of dead grass and flexible roots. When he gets to the storeroom, he pushes with his forelimbs, beginning at the rear, so that the food comes out of the cheek pockets like toothpaste being squeezed from a tube.

Prairie dogs run for their burrows when a falcon with outstretched claws drops swiftly from above.

The seasons move across the vast sea of grass, and the prairie changes from green to brown to white. It gives little hint of the big populations of diggers that live successfully beneath its surface—prairie dogs, ground squirrels, burrowing owls, marmots, mice, badgers, and gophers. The prairie is a world mostly of the unseen.

Dark fingers of the giant saguaro cactus reach 50 feet up into the sky. When storage chambers are full of water, after a heavy rain, the huge plants may weigh as much as 10 tons.

Desert Miracles

LAND teeming with life is green. So with the tundra in summer, the mountain stronghold, and even the grassy prairie. But the desert floor is white in the glare of sunlight. Its narrow valleys are drowned in blue haze. Slopes are streaked with black sand or black rock from ancient lava flows. The flat-topped mountains are purple, red, yellow, and pink.

These are the colors of raw elements, the spectrum of pure sunlight. These were the colors of the land before plants grew on the hot earth's crust, before animals came out of the sea to live on green leaves, fruits, and seeds—to run on grass and hide in the forest.

Some of the deserts in our Southwest were created when the mountains of California were pushed up and caused rain-bearing clouds from the Pacific Ocean to drop their moisture before

A tiny elf owl—no bigger than a songbird—has pecked out a comfortable home high up in a giant saguaro cactus.

it reached far inland. With little rain, desert land can show but little green. And with little plant life, there can be little animal life.

The pioneers loved the prairie and even the mountains, but when they saw the desert, they shuddered. They ventured across fingers of the desert on Indian trails connecting the few scattered streams and water holes, but they shunned the rest.

DEATH VALLEY

In one place the heart of the desert—Death Valley—lay directly across their path. The valley lies along the east side of the Sierras under the rain shadow of Mount Whitney, the highest point in the United States. A "rain shadow" is just the opposite of what it sounds like: there is no shadow, no rain. The mountains catch the air-borne moisture from the Pacific and store it up in deep snow fields. At Death Valley the rain shadow is deepest, and so this is the driest place in our country, and the lowest—280 feet below sea level. For days without a break, the thermometer may stay around 120°. In July 1913 it hit 134°, the record high on earth. All this within eighty miles of snow fields!

The pioneers crossed Death Valley as a short cut to California during the gold rush of 1849. Many died of thirst and heat. But they did not give up the search for gold and for something far more valuable—water.

Salt flats, glaring in the sun, mark places where lakes disappeared into the sand long ago. But in Death Valley a spring was discovered. Named Stove Pipe, after the piece of rusty hardware left by a pioneer to mark the spot, it saved many lives. One prospector, Two-Gun, saw to it that a shovel was always left beside the stove pipe so that a thirsty traveler could dig out the spring from under the drifting sand.

The Great American Desert stretches for hundreds of miles between the massive ranges of the Sierra Nevada and the Rockies.

Spines of the barrel cactus guard the plant's precious stores of water. Many thirsty desert travelers have stopped to tap these plants and drink. In the background is a grove of thorny, low-growing mesquite.

Instead of finding gold in Death Valley, prospectors found a cleansing and antiseptic salt called borax. Someone thought up the famous twenty-mule-team wagon, and soon it was crunching over the oven floor of Death Valley like a freight train. Driven by one man on a high seat, the wagon was pulled by ten pairs of mules. Sometimes the animals would go mad for water, and there would be a chaos of rattling harness chains. Behind the wagon, a trailer carrying big water barrels was followed by a disgruntled group of spare mules—reserve power to get the outfit over ninety miles of desert.

THE STONE TREES

The desert is very old, and among the signs of its great age are the bodies of large trees sprawled here and there. From a distance, they look as though they had just been felled. Some are 150 feet long; others, quite short. A few are light-colored, like pine wood. But these logs would make a poor campfire, for they are solid stone, mostly agate, with the brilliant colors of the rainbow.

Once upon a time these trees grew in a swampy forest. That was about 160 million years ago—before the Sierras rose and made the desert. The trees were of a kind that no longer grow in our country. In that forest lived crocodiles eighteen feet long and giant salamanders weighing five hundred pounds. In the forest ponds were fishes that breathed with lungs instead of gills—fishes whose teeth are today found among the stone logs.

As the mountains rose up in the west and the desert formed, the forest withered away. But some of the old tree trunks were preserved as ancient streams buried them in mud, sand, and salt. The trunks rotted away, bit by bit, and water percolating through them left bits of mineral to replace the rotted parts. The trunks thus slowly changed to stone. Later, running water and wind removed the earth above them and exposed them for us to see today.

MIRACLES OF DESERT LIFE

The desert looks as if nothing could live there. So the pioneers thought when they were blinded by glare and tortured with thirst while crossing Death Valley. They heard no sound of life, saw nothing moving except "dust devils"—tiny whirlwinds which run across the desert and suddenly disappear like ghosts.

But on higher ground, above the salt flats at the bottom, grows a strange plant that was one of the first attempts of nature to make something alive out of sunshine shining on hot sand. Mormon tea, or the Ephedra bush, looks like nothing more than a few straight leafless twigs attached to a heavy stick. This queer old bush proved that plants can live in the desert if they don't try to look and act like ordinary plants.

Elsewhere plants depend on having water all the time, whether from rain or ground water. Ordinary plants, growing in normally moist soil, operate as water-lifting machines. They grow fast and big, making food, circulating sap, and discarding water through their leaves.

To live on the desert, a plant must be able to live on very little water and to wait for it—months or years if need be. Such a plant must not evaporate it into the air. It must have roots long enough to tap moisture far below the surface. The root cells must be able to hold moisture and also to act instantly to pick up water near the surface of the desert when rain does come. Finally, desert plants must contain airtight, watertight storage tanks.

The ugly Mormon tea plant has no leaves. Its chlorophyll, for food-making, is in the stems. These do not lose water, because they are sealed with quartz crystals from the sand. In other words, the plant is covered with glass, which lets the light reach the chlorophyll. This weird bush grows so slowly and irregularly that it can hardly be seen to change size at all.

Sagebrush, a member of the thistle family, came over from the prairie to pepper parts of the desert with deep-plunging roots. Its little leaves are covered with wool to keep their surfaces shady and hold whatever moisture there is in the air.

Greasewood is a member of the pigweed family that also learned the trick of deep roots. The little leaves of greasewood are thick and waterproof. They seal in water instead of letting it escape through holes.

The creosote bush, related to rubber trees, is an astonishing desert success. Its little green leaves look all the brighter because they are covered with resin that seals up their water.

NEITHER TREE, NOR BUSH, NOR FLOWER

The greatest plant miracle here is the cactus, which seems to be neither tree, nor bush, nor wildflower. All cactuses grow differently and look different from other plants.

The pincushion cactus is round. The barrel cactus is barrel-shaped. The prickly-pear cactus is the shape of pancakes stuck together at their edges. The organ-pipe cactus, just as its name indicates, consists of big pipes going straight up. The living-rock cactus has projections and humps, exactly as though carved out of one of the stones among which it grows.

The teddy-bear cactus, also called cholla, looks soft and fluffy. The soft fluffiness comes off in clusters of sharp needles. When you try to pull them off, they stick painfully—and persistently—into your fingers.

The bobcat has the miraculous ability to climb over the cruel thorns of the giant saguaro.

GREATEST OF ALL

The greatest cactus of all, the biggest living thing on the desert, is the saguaro. The whole cactus may be in the form of a giant candelabrum, with arms coming out at the same height and turning up. The plant may rise forty feet without an arm. The arms may bend at the elbow as though beckoning, or turn at crazy angles as though stuck on by a joker.

The outside shell is rich green and smoothly waxed with resin, which makes it watertight. The shell does the job of leaves in making food out of sunlight, water, and earth. Deep parallel ridges run along each arm, with vicious thorns closely spaced along the crests. These ridges look tough and rigid, but they can fold and unfold like an accordion.

This green tower is a reservoir for water. When a downpour comes, the plant expands to hold more water. In a long dry spell, the pleats fold in and the plant shrinks.

Sooner or later it will rain, probably quite heavily. Half the rain of a whole year may fall in one night. The next morning, the surface sand is dry, the pools have vanished, the stream beds are dry and eroded-looking again. But the saguaro was prepared. Its roots are spread flat and wide, as a big water-collecting net, just below the surface in the sand.

Saguaro roots remain idle for months, seemingly baked to cinders in the sand—then go into action the moment they feel the touch of water. They keep on collecting as long as the wetness is there. One cloudburst may fill the plant so full that it can last on its personal water supply through four years of drought.

The greatest danger to a saguaro would be a continuous water supply, for this plant has no way of stopping its own intake of water. Let the desert turn into a wet place and the saguaro would fatten to its limit, explode, and die.

The saguaro stops its leaks ingeniously. Its spongy, pithy cells are tiny water bags with thin walls through which the water seeps. The outer cells contain a sticky substance like mucilage. When the outside shell is punctured, the mucilage is touched by air, hardens, and coats the inside of the hole—stopping the leak.

The saguaro has one more problem to solve: standing upright. A fifty-foot plant may weigh six tons. So the saguaro must have a strong skeleton. This is formed by a framework of hardened cells running the whole length of the trunk. These cells are buried in the water cells just beneath the outer shell.

The resin that makes the skeleton also makes the sharp thorns. These are some of the tough-

The ocotillo (center) is not a cactus. It drops its leaves in dry spells, and releafs when it rains. True cactus—like the prickly pear at left and the cholla at right—have no leaves whatever.

est plant material ever created. They do not disintegrate when scorched endlessly by the sun, and are practically unbreakable. Their colors—bright red, pink, purple, yellow, orange, brown, and white—are very attractive.

DESERT TOM

The bobcat lives among the trees and ledges of the canyons. He's a night runner that loves to pounce on little animals which come out when all is cool and dark. He goes up the saguaro after woodpecker eggs, or just to rest up there and scan the desert floor.

How can the bobcat run up over the saguaro's ruthless thorns? He has some way of dealing with sharp things. Perhaps the pads under his toes are puncture-proof. Or else he places his feet so as to push against the sides of the prickers instead of their points.

In January and February, when calling for a mate, the cat may pierce the quiet night with caterwauling worse than any you hear on a back fence in the city. Let wood rats, jack rabbits, lizards, toads, turtles, kangaroo rats—and all the company that pop out from underground and run around the desert at night—beware! Yet he is more dangerous when he travels silently.

When the cat meets prey that puts up a good fight, he forgets all about strategy and becomes an animal typhoon. He screams, spits, hisses, and scratches.

The fight with a bobcat is quickly over. Fortunately for the other animals, this aggressor in the desert is only after a meal. When that is eaten, he retires to his haunts in the canyon.

The big population of little desert diggers, on the other hand, do not disturb the peace by fighting among themselves. They are out of sight in daytime, when most great animal fighting takes place. When they come out at night, they walk and hop on the desert's vast expanse. They are not apt to bump into each other, for they are little and the desert very big. At dawn, they once more vanish into holes.

The Joshua tree is the largest member of the yucca family. Its strange haphazard patterns are a familiar feature of the desert scene.

Kangaroo rats emerge from their burrows only at night—instantly ready to hop away to safety on their long powerful, kangaroo-like hind legs.

PYGMY KANGAROOS

The kangaroo rat of the American desert is a handsome mouse, about twelve inches long from nose to tail tip. About seven inches of that is a long strong tail, with a brush at the end that acts as a balance for the rest of the body and as a rudder when sailing through the air. When he puts his heart into it, the mouse can clear eight feet of hot sand—more, in proportion to size, than the giant kangaroo can do in Australia.

Some of the bigger kinds of kangaroo rats dwell in the driest, hottest heart of the desert—Death Valley. They *never take a drink*.

How can this be? A camel may go a month without water because it has an extra stomach which holds gallons of water in reserve. A desert toad, buried like a living mummy under the sand, can live off its own blood forty-six weeks or more. Seeds of plants live for years in their waterproof coats. But sooner or later all these living things must renew their supply of water by taking a good drink, or they die. Why not the kangaroo rat?

This little fellow not only had his limbs redesigned for desert jumping, but also had his insides redesigned to perform a chemical miracle. He nibbles on the driest seeds and on dead stems; he does not even have to eat anything damp, like a leaf.

DESERT-STYLED ANIMALS

A rabbit is the color of gray sand and stones, and he comes with long hind legs for jumping. But the form of his body makes him sit high and in that position he can't eat. To nibble on grass and seeds among the stones on the desert floor, he must put his head away down. His fine big eyes may then miss a hawk, coyote, or fox sneaking up. But nature has pulled the desert rabbit's ears far out. When his head is down, the super-tall ears stick straight up—tuned in on the surrounding desert.

The horned lizard (which people call a "toad," although it isn't) goes for ants and caterpillars on the ground. Accordingly its own face is near the ground. Its wide, flat body, colored and spotted like the desert floor, is almost invisible. In case a snake does come upon it, the horned lizard is armed with spines and prickles, reminders of the untouchable cactus.

The desert is full of things that seem to call for the wildest imagination. One is the Gila

The king snake is a friend to man because of the many rodents he eats. But he is the kangaroo rat's chief enemy.

If this kangaroo rat recovers from fright before the sidewinder strikes, he will scratch sand into the snake's eyes, and make his escape.

monster (pronounced "heela monster"). This lizard, about a foot and a half long, lies in the sunflecked shade of a creosote bush, fat and limp as a sack of grain. He drags himself along slowly, looking for centipedes and millipedes which run past on little legs that follow each other like the wheels of a long freight train. A quick motion and the train disappears. The lizard lets the centipedes and millipedes roll along, however, when he catches sight of snake or lizard eggs.

The Gila monster was converted into a desert model by being covered with a beautiful piece of natural insulation. This consists of many tiny bones, rounded on top like polished beads. These are bright salmon pink, yellow, white, and jet black, in designs like Navajo Indian beadwork. They make the monster almost sunproof. If he lies in the thin shade of a bush, perhaps that is because he can find more centipedes and millipedes there!

MORNING ON THE DESERT

By the time the sun is above the mesa on the eastern horizon, the desert's various night runners are under the sand. Now the daylight squads suddenly appear. They will be in more of a hurry than the others, who had all night. In an hour, it will be too hot to hunt. But the night runners will have another chance when the sun is low in the west.

The desert rabbit sits beside a stone, his tall ears straight up as he jerks his head around to get a good listen of the new day. The little gray lizard is at the edge of a mesquite shadow, stretching up to see what goes on out there where the sun is brightening the sand. Suddenly the face of a young rattlesnake is caught by the daylight at the entrance to a little cave. He opens his mouth wide as though enjoying a fangy yawn after a good night's sleep.

High above, at a dark hole in a saguaro, another face appears. A woodpecker surveys the desert. He has made an air-conditioned room for himself in the saguaro. His technique was to drill around the thorns until they fell off.

Lacking a true tree, the cactus wren chooses the thick, writhing arms of the cholla cactus. His house must have floor, walls, and roof, and how he does the whole thing among a hundred stabbing spears is a wonder. Working furiously, he somehow gets a mass of material for the nest wedged down among the spines.

THE RUNNING MACHINE

Rabbit, lizard, and rattlesnake jump to attention when something that resembles a long-legged hen sprints between two creosote bushes. This "hen," really the roadrunner cuckoo, is a creature of the desert as truly as the kangaroo rat. He gets all his water from meat. He can build a nest in a cholla next to the cactus wren, or in a thorny mesquite or any other thorny scrub. His speed is dazzling. He runs

The roadrunner—a kind of cuckoo—is one of the few creatures quick enough to outwit a rattlesnake. Darting and feinting, he tires the snake, finally pecks out his eyes and eats him.

across a gap here, and over there, and suddenly he is far away.

The roadrunner can fly a short distance, in a sort of extended bounce. His wings are short and round, designed to send him over the desert fast by taking weight off his feet. He spreads his wings and sails right over cactuses, mesquites, and creosote bushes. His powerful muscles favor his legs. He runs entirely on tiptoe, with heels bent back and held high. Knees and thighs, short and buried in the body feathers, work like strong springs, the upper part of the legs vibrating with short fast strokes while the feet take long strides.

THE TAIL OF THE LIZARD

The little gray lizard, a champion runner himself, can flex his body and swing his long tail so as to swerve, turn sharply, double back without changing pace, and elude capture by almost any pursuer. But the roadrunner is the world's most expert twister and turner.

If the roadrunner grabs the lizard's tail, this may break off, allowing the lizard to escape. (The lizard will grow another tail later—not as good, but useful enough.) But the lizard will probably end up in a nest in a cholla, there to be swallowed headfirst by a baby roadrunner. The young bird, beginning with the head, chews slowly, and the tail of the lizard—if any—will droop from its mouth for a long time.

ROADRUNNER VERSUS RATTLESNAKE

What should a rattlesnake fear? When it moves into the burrow of a kangaroo rat or a rabbit, the owner moves out fast—if it can. When the snake comes out in the morning to lie in the sun, all the neighbors keep at a safe distance. Nothing on the desert dares to challenge the dictatorship of the rattlesnake—except the long-tailed, cactus-crested roadrunner!

The roadrunner regularly eats centipedes, grasshoppers, bugs, crickets, and spiders. But one day he feels like a change. He lifts his tail straight up and drills a rattler with a look from his round, bright eyes. The rattler lifts his head high, and in his open mouth the tongue quivers. He coils and gives a dry, menacing rattle.

The sidewinder rattlesnake is named for his peculiar sidewise movement. It leaves odd, discontinuous tracks in his wake in the sand.

The female pepsis wasp is called the "tarantula hawk" because she is the spider's deadliest enemy. In desperate struggles like this one, the wasp usually wins, paralyzing the spider with her poisoned sting.

His strike is so swift it's invisible, and a prick from the pair of deadly needles would finish the roadrunner. Yet the snake is outmaneuvered from the start. The roadrunner dances around, keeping always just out of reach. He dodges the deadly fangs—teases the snake to go on striking into thin air. At last the head of the snake wavers, its strike becomes feeble. The bird swiftly closes in. Two pecks, one in each eye, and it's all over.

The hungry roadrunner swallows the limp rattlesnake head first. A leisurely dinner—inch by inch—has begun.

THE TARANTULA AND THE WASP

When the egg of a pepsis wasp hatches, the new little larva needs something to eat. In fact, it needs fresh tarantula meat. But a tarantula is a monster – big, hairy, powerful, with poison fangs that spell death. And how can tarantula meat be kept fresh for ten days in desert temperatures? If the meat is the least spoiled, the baby wasp will die.

The mother pepsis wasp has the answer, and she goes forth to hunt a tarantula.

The tarantula's castle is a burrow about an inch wide and a foot deep, lined with silk to prevent sand and stones from falling out of the sides and also to give footholds for climbing. Here the spider spends most of its time, four of its eight eyes gleaming alertly in the dark. (The other four don't gleam.) The top of the hole is surrounded by a parapet about an inch high. On this the tarantula may sit motionless, waiting for crawling prey, such as a beetle, to come along. From the parapet, the tarantula can leap down and strike.

The wasp must wait until she can catch the hairy monster up there in the open. If she can get her needle into just the right spot and inject just the right amount of poison, her victim will be not killed, but paralyzed. That is a wasp's substitution for refrigeration. The right spot is the nerve center on the hairy chest of the tarantula. For the wasp to reach that, the spider must be walking on its eight legs, instead of having them folded over its thorax.

When her chance comes, the slender wasp, antennae and wings quivering, charges the spider. She grips its hairy corselet with her jaws

Around the base of its single shaft of white lilies, the yucca grows a clump of dagger-sharp leaves.

and tries to swing herself up. When astride the monster, she can curve her abdomen and slip the end of it under the spider's thorax, driving in the needle at exactly the right spot.

The spider has a target of its own—an exposed spot on the neck of the wasp. It rears like a bronco and throws off the wasp. They spar. One thrusts with its face, the other backs into action. The wasp jumps high, buzzes its wings, tries to dive onto the back of the spider. The spider feints with its abdomen, then suddenly sidesteps.

After a while, the big tarantula is lying on its back, quivering. The wasp has grasped the spider, but she can drag this enormous load only a short distance. Soon she drops it and digs furiously. Then she grabs a leg, pulls and hauls, folds and pushes, until the tarantula is all tucked into the hole.

The wasp now lays one egg. She glues it to a certain spot on the spider's breast. The spider can move its legs in its sleep, but at this spot the egg is bound to be safe.

The work of the pepsis wasp is completed; she has done it well.

THE LITTLE WHITE GHOST AND THE LILY

Where higher ground above the desert floor folds into a canyon, the sand is studded with bunches of bayonets. Some emerge from a point on the ground and stick out in all directions as if from pincushions. Others grow on Joshua trees, which have balls of bayonets radiating from the ends of big writhing branches lifted some twenty feet high on heavy trunks.

Both are yucca lilies. Although the leaves are long and slender, like ordinary lily leaves, they are thickened for water storage and are airproofed with wax. In the spring a mighty stem comes forth from the pincushions, quickly grows to heights of from two to ten feet, and releases a skyrocket of white lilies. White lilies also burst from the Joshua trees. This is a miracle that has been understood only in recent years.

One night, when yucca lilies open and release their wonderful fragrance on the desert air, little white ghosts appear among them. These are pronuba moths, which have been months underground, wrapped up like small mummies. The flowers' fragrance pulls them like magnets in the darkness.

The female pronuba moth makes straight for stamens bursting with pollen. She scrapes together a wad of pollen exactly three times bigger than her head. Holding this load with her mouth, she flies to another yucca plant. Still holding the ball of pollen, she backs down to the bottom of the flower, drills a hole with her egg-laying needle, and deposits a clutch of moth eggs inside the green pod at the base of the pistil. Next she climbs to the top of the same pistil, where there is a cavity exactly three times bigger than her head. She stuffs in the wad of pollen, which fits perfectly. Nature does the rest.

While the pronuba eggs are getting ready to hatch, the yucca's seeds are ripening. When the moth's larvae come into the world, they find themselves surrounded with their special kind of food—green yucca seeds, all moist and fresh. They do not eat all of the great numbers of seeds in the pod; they leave plenty of extra seeds to raise more yuccas—and more pronuba moths, too.

Where did the pronuba learn the art of plant breeding? What inspired her to drive home the right amount of pollen in the right spot? How can it be that she does everything in the right order? The desert keeps all the answers secret.

The low-growing beavertail cactus is free of thorns. Instead, the joints of its stems are pitted and pocked.

THE FLOWERING DESERT

During months, perhaps years, the desert does not change its appearance. The air is pure, the sky blue, white clouds sit on distant mountains. Cactuses, mesquite, creosote bushes, and sage stand without changing color or size, as though painted on the desert floor. Everything can wait —it doesn't seem to matter when the rain comes. But when some day the rain does come, a magical spectacle may be seen.

Countless billions of seeds have been scattered invisibly across the sand. Each contains the germ of a poppy flower, packed with a tiny bit of moisture, in a sunproof case. These sparks of life wait in the desert.

Now the rain comes, and the sand is soaked and cooled, and this buried life suddenly awakens. A bright red and yellow carpet unrolls across the desert. Nothing on earth can match the splendor of the desert at this hour. This is the miracle of our desert world.

The giant saguaro, growing only in the southern part of the state, is Arizona's state flower.

The prickly pear cactus produces reddish-brown edible fruits, after its golden flowers wither.

Secret worlds of wonder are to be found in this peaceful acre. Butterflies and birds, squirrels and trees, and untold thousands of plants and insects make it a paradise—and a battleground.

Big Adventures in Little Worlds

EVERY summer morning, a curtain of light shoots over the horizon at sunrise and sweeps across the ground. Countless living things that have been stowed away in secret hiding places during the night instantly respond in a great variety of ways. The taller flowers, which are touched first by the sun and the quick breeze that travels with the light, jerk open their buds and revolve their petals. Bees pop out of the hollow tree and buzz around in ever-widening circles, scouting for the flowers to be raided that day.

As the shadows brighten under a tree, there is a little liquid plop on the glassy surface of a pool where a frog dives in—with arms and legs extended like those of a tiny naked green boy. Above in the tree a woolly-bear caterpillar ripples along a branch, en route to its hunting ground on the leaves. Wet grass blades quiver and their dewdrops fall where an eft scampers through, looking for a piece of damp shade in a hurry. A wren gives a repeated trill like a little electric bell. A phoebe swings back and forth on the floppy topmost branch of a juniper tree, jerking its tail vigorously and sweetly saying "*Phoebe*" over and over again.

SECRET WORLDS AROUND US

It is morning in the little worlds, and astonishing adventures await us when we explore them. Life here in tunnels in the ground, in the hidden machinery of flowers, in beehives, in trees, in fresh-water ponds, in seaweed jungles between the tides, in a drop of water—is more miraculous and startling in reality than any thing we could dream up as living on other planets.

We usually see trees and flowers as fixtures of our landscape. When we peer closely, we discover that they have made miniatures of themselves, complete with leaf, stem, and root. These seeds—little images of the mother tree or flower—a small fraction of an inch in size, are tightly packed parcels, wrapped in weatherproof coats. And they possess a peculiar power to go places and plant themselves. They may fly, walk, or even burrow into the ground.

Look again into the secrets of plants. Although plants cannot run around when they have taken root, some can catch lively prey for dinner. They do not pursue, but they outsmart the insects. The plant lies in wait with a trap baited with fantastic colors and odors. Insects that are lured to touch its leaves cannot escape, and the plant has a feast.

The animals of the hiding places of nature stagger the imagination. Their bodies are often

A red-spotted butterfly, poised on a daisy, drinks nectar with his tube-shaped mouth.

In early spring, brooks are busy carrying off the melted snows of winter, while in every bush and tree the sap is rising.

transparent; some display sparkling colors. They have all sorts of queer shapes, and some—compared to man—have titanic strength for their size. Some can run or fly faster than the eye can follow. Some, with microscopic heads, have ways of communication that are beyond our understanding. Some can multiply faster than we can count.

The secret worlds make a book of countless chapters, through which runs the rhythm of the seasons, the story of earth changing, of plants and animals struggling to live on, of living things dying and making life possible for living things to come.

In spring the sun crosses the sky a little higher each day. It sprays its tiny energy bullets against the earth more and more directly, closer and closer together. The increasing sun bullets strike trees, lakes, rocks, and earth and set off a billion tiny events. Grains of ice and snow fade away, and trickles of water grow noisier in the woodlands. Crystal fingers of frost melt in the soil and leave it tunneled, damp, and airy-ready for green heads of seeds to thrust through from below. Sun bullets hitting buds start the chemical magic by which air, water, and minerals become leaves, tree trunks, and flowers.

The sun bullets strike hard. The tiniest particles of gases that make up our air get battered into swifter motion. The tiniest particles that make up water, rock, and soil also move faster. Earth becomes warm.

Plants now send out new roots and spread their leaves to begin taking in chemical foods. Animals that have slept through the winter wake up to join the hustle, and those that have hungered during the lean months now begin to eat well. Birds announce their arrival from the south, eggs hatch, and wet butterflies crawl forth. The land and its inhabitants, plant and animal, are now full of activity. It doesn't happen all in a day, but there is a day when you know that summer has come.

After a few months, when the sun is lower in the sky again, little walls begin to form between the twigs of trees and their leaf stems. The leaves can get no more sap to drink, and they put on their funeral colors as the pace of life slows down. One morning a glistening white powder shows on the leaves that used to hold sparkling little balls of water after cool nights. Jack Frost has passed by, and you know he will soon come to stay.

In summertime all life is quickened—plants thrive, insects hum in the meadows and animals grow strong in the heat and brilliance of the sun.

With the coming of fall the tempo of life gradually slows. Animals store food for winter, and leaves fall and die,covering the hills with a blaze of color.

In winter the land and its creatures rest. Wrapped in cold and snow, animals sleep, and plant life waits for the warmth and sunshine of another spring.

The shoreline is constantly being ground down and worn away by the pounding waves.

But winter is only a season. It is only a slowing down for those plants and animals—oaks and bears and all the rest—that will stir and hustle again when the sun rides higher. It is only a phase for those short-lived individuals that will die when the world freezes, but have left parts of themselves—seeds and eggs and buried larvae—to begin new lives when the earth warms

Ages ago the body of this fish was buried in mud that slowly hardened, under pressure, to form rock. Scientists have learned much about prehistoric times from studying similar petrified casts and other fossils.

again. It is as if they knew that even in winter the earth, in all its secret places, under the rocks and ice and leaves and snow, will be making ready.

THE MIXING BOWL OF LIFE

So far as we know, the sea was the home of the first living things, the algae and trilobites and ancient fishes. It is still the home of all sorts of life, from the tiny single-celled animals to our mammal cousins, the whales. But that is not all. Besides covering most of the earth, the sea is always at work on the remainder.

The surf beats upon the edges of the land, gradually wearing and breaking them into the smallest grains. From the ocean, the sun's heat

When Mauna Loa in Hawaii erupted, curtains of steam filled the sky as the bubbling lava plunged into the sea.

lifts billions of tons of water into the upper air. Condensing into clouds, the moisture is swept across the land as rain, and eventually finds its way back to the ocean down the long winding trails of rivers.

Every drop of water that falls on the land leaves its trace. Billions of drops become frost to split the rocks and break up the soil. Other billions join with chemicals in air and soil to eat away the stone hills, grain by grain. Still other billions join in armies to rush down the slopes and gouge their way to the sea. It is as if the sea were determined to drag every last bit of land down into itself.

Yet the sea also builds land. Countless bits of stone carried by rivers drift down to the sea bottoms along with a slow rain of dead animals, plants, and other sea wastes. There they pile up, layer upon layer, sometimes mile upon mile, squeezed harder and harder by their own weight. At last they have become stone. The ocean floor itself may sink beneath this enormous weight. But sooner or later some spasm in the earth's crust is likely to heave these layers of new rock above the waves. A few million years more, and this old sea bottom, the dark green home of creatures that never saw the sun, has become the windswept mountain hideout of the bighorn and the panther, flanked by sunny valleys in which birds and muskrats and land life in all its variety go busily about their affairs as if the world had always been this way.

The earth—this great ball of gases, water, rock, and soil—is a restless, trembling thing. Deep in the planet, rocks that have been heated by radioactivity and mashed by miles of earth above them, are a white-hot liquid, frantically pressing to escape in any direction. As the great stone blocks that form the earth's crust shift slowly up and down, like wood blocks bobbing in water, cracks open up here and there, and the white-hot rock rushes upward through them to burst out of the earth if it can. It may burst out through a mountain, a plain, or even the ocean floor; and we have a new volcano.

For millions of years the earth has been casting up liquid rock from its depths and pouring it across our upper world. This melted rock, or lava, so terrible-appearing when it erupts from the fiery craters of volcanoes, cools before

As lava cools, a black crust forms on its surface. In years to come it will become some of the earth's most fertile soil.

Under tremendous pressures, lava sometimes bursts through the earth's crust, shooting up into the air like great rockets of fire.

it can flow far. Soon it is wearing away under the attack of wind and water, and eventually it becomes fine, rich soil—a paradise for plant and animal populations.

Even living things help to prepare the land. Remains of dead plants and animals are scattered over the ground and become mixed with bits of sand, clay, and other minerals to form fertile soil. Earthworms bore through this soil, opening it to the air. When beavers build their dams, the flow of water through soil may be changed for miles around. The leaves of trees shade the soil and prevent too much of its moisture from being stolen by the sun; and the roots of trees hold water that might otherwise run down slopes or trickle deep into the earth and be quickly lost.

THE DARK CAVERNS

If you clasp a seed in your hand, it will not grow. But in the quiet, dark soil, it begins to move and to develop beautiful forms and colors.

Rainstorms bring water, which is stored up underground, between irregularly shaped grains of soil.

This tells us the soil possesses its own magic—a secret of life.

What we call dirt seems solid under our feet. But that is a great misunderstanding. One of the wonders of soil is that it is not solid at all. Grains of sediment are irregular, jagged shapes of different sizes, and do not fit tightly together. Pieces touch at countless points, making the ground firm; but spaces are everywhere between them.

In some places more than half the soil consists of spaces filled with air and water. The secret power of soil is in the spaces between grains. Think of the spaces as a vast system of connecting caves. The tiny soil animals and bacteria in the caves between the grains do not miss the sun. They spend their lives in the darkness of the jungles of root hairs, and get the energy of the sun indirectly. It comes to them as food from larger animals that go up into the world of sunlight part of the time, and return to the soil to live and die. Sun energy is also packed into leaves, twigs, and fruits. These fall and decay, and their energy is absorbed into the soil.

Rushing streams erode the hills and rocks, and build up fertile soils on the floors of the valleys.

Soil spaces are air-conditioned. They never get too hot or too cold. There is always plenty of water. This may be in pools in the spaces where it is trapped. But usually the spaces of living soil do not hold water for long, because after a rain the water trickles down through the spaces. Most water is held as a shiny coating on the surfaces of grains of soil. There is so much invisible water in the air underground that the Weather Bureau would say it is on the point of raining—at 100 percent humidity.

The things that live in the soil never go hungry. There is always plenty of food at hand. Soil is the world's mixing bowl; it brings together all the elements life needs, cooks them, and makes them ready for all the billions of plant roots that must feed on them.

THE WONDER OF ROOTS

Of all the strange events that take place in the zigzagging caverns of the soil, the most surprising are the travels of the roots and the threads that burst out from their tips. They are the fastest-growing and the longest part of the plant. A scientist measured the area of the roots and hairs of a single plant of winter rye, and found that they had a surface one hundred times greater than all the parts that grew above the ground.

Even more unbelievable was the speed with which they lengthened. Three miles of new roots grew each day. Those are the regular roots—the brown, stringy ones. Added to them are billions of microscopic white root hairs that

Within the space of a few hours, a raging forest fire can destroy an entire forest.

slide through spaces between grains of soil. With these added, the rate of root travel of this single plant of winter rye averaged the astounding total of neary fifty-three miles per day.

In all the wonders of life nothing is more marvelous than this power drive of roots through the soil. How can a thing as slender and soft as a thread penetrate the soil that seems so compact? What is the mechanism that makes their extended travels possible?

The root wears a hard little helmet at its point. This acts as a wedge. It is pushed forward with half a pound of pressure, and when inserted between grains of soil, expands with eight pounds of pressure. The tip controls the activity, thrusting and steering the course, guiding the root in its twistings and turnings. It goes toward wetter ground and avoids the drier. It detours around larger stones and the root follows it like a snake, taking the easiest path.

We think of roots as we see them when a tree is blown over—heavy, brown, crooked wood from which brown strings dangle. This

Yet even while the ashes are warm the seeds of new trees are planted, and a new forest begins to rise.

The worm snake is one of the soil's little diggers. It makes its home in burrows, feeding on insect larvae, ant pupae, and termites.

is the anchor part. It forces its way between cracks of rocks, if it must, without any sign of disturbing the soil.

But the roots which touch the life-giving magic of the soil are not tough, heavy, and brown. They are white hairs as fine as the silk of a spider web. Each has a point as sharp as a needle. The helmet at the tip of the growing root has butted and wedged its way forward and discovered fresh caves between the soil grains, with walls glistening with water. Then these hairs spring out from the root just behind the helmeted tip. Water acts on the root hairs like a magnet. Billions of thirsty threads poke into every space. When one touches a grain of sand coated with water, it spreads like a tiny baseball mitt to take hold of the grain and soak up the water.

Earthworms eat their way through the loam, aerating the soil with the tunnels they leave behind.

AN UNDERGROUND POWERHOUSE

The soil is a storage battery, a powerhouse of energy which is first delivered to the earth as sunlight. Scientists tell us that the energy which comes to the whole earth is more than four hundred million-million horsepower a day. A large part of the sun's energy is caught by green leaves, where it is stored. When autumn comes, the leaves turn brown and die. The wind sweeps them from the trees. They fall to earth and decay in the soil where their locked-up energy is set free, to be used by life underground.

THE LITTLE DIGGERS

Many little animals that are much bigger than the soil animals have discovered that the soil is a good place to live. They do not fit into the spaces between grains. They must dig to get into the soil.

All across the land, insects are rushing in and out of the soil. Some use unbelievable strength to push aside pebbles, sticks, and balls of earth when climbing out to reach the light.

Ants keep their exits and entrances always open. These are round holes as cleanly formed as man's tunnels. But ant holes are usually under leaves, sticks, or fallen pieces of bark. These keep raindrops from falling into the holes.

While ants carry soil, ball by ball, out of their tunnels and pile it up in neat little ant hills, earthworms make equally fine tunnels in an entirely different way. The earthworm moves

Many beetles make their home in the earth. This ground beetle has just robbed an ant of its prey.

forward by swallowing the soil which its head meets. Mouthfuls of soil particles, with all the soil animals and bacteria in them, slide through the body of an earthworm as through a little rubber hose, coming out at the other end as the earthworm moves ahead. When the earthworm breaks through the surface, it keeps hold of the opening of its tunnel with one end of its body and stretches out like a rubber band, looking for bits of dead leaves and twigs to eat. This blind animal of the dark soil is ready to snap back into its hole the instant it is alarmed by an enemy.

WORLD'S GREATEST DIGGERS

Ants are the world's greatest diggers, and far outnumber all other diggers. They keep busy running their underground tunnels.

The ant is famous for the network of tiny caverns it digs in the ground. This ant will carry the captured termite into its underground storehouse.

Prairie dogs build a maze of underground tunnels—where they can escape from coyotes and eagles.

Rabbits hide their young in burrows in the earth until they are old enough to run swiftly from danger.

Ants all do their running around in the daylight and go home at night. When an ant queen drops down from her marriage flight in strange territory, she immediately starts digging. In this way, she is beginning a new colony that may have a hundred thousand ants in a few years.

Ant tunnels are clean, round tubes, narrower than a pencil. They are carefully built to last for years. To start a tunnel, an ant first clamps its jaws closed and uses them like a trowel. The jaws stick out a little, and when closed they are curved and pointed at the tip. The ant digs and scrapes with this trowel and molds and presses the dirt with it. Later the swiftly passing, polished bodies of ants will smooth the inside of the tunnel.

When roots get in the way, the ant uses its jaws to snip them off. If pebbles block the way, the jaws close on them and they are carried outdoors. The ant does not throw the waste from its diggings into a pile but scatters it far and wide to conceal the little hole until there has been time to fortify the entrance.

Ants use their tunnels to get to the halls and rooms where they lay eggs, store food, and sometimes cultivate an indoor garden. Halls, irregular and narrow, are used mostly for communication between rooms. They allow a lot of ants working at the same time in great excitement to carry their eggs and babies from one room to another if an enemy turns up. The rooms have flat floors and arched ceilings.

The underground homes of ants are enlarged through the years. Some of the oldest, with an almost endless series of mysterious galleries and rooms, may house several hundred thousand. This is called a colony, but it is actually a family, because most of the ants are the children of one queen.

However, ant queens do not battle as queen bees do, so ant nests may contain several families living together. They must all smell the same way, and the smell makes them feel comfortable together. Also the family odor is paid out along their trails when they run outside. No matter how many different ant trails crisscross and get mixed up outdoors, each ant finds its way back to its own family by following the familiar odor trail.

The ant can vanish fast. In the house it darts into the nearest crack. Outdoors it dodges under a leaf or stone so fast that you don't know where it went. If you step near an ant hill swarming with ants, they disappear as though blown away by a puff of wind.

The badger, too, makes his home underground. He feeds on mice, squirrels, and quail, and can even dig prairie dogs out of their holes.

THE BIG DIGGERS

It seems as though the nearest animals ever come to smiling is when they are sitting beside, or peering up at you from, a hole in the ground. Why not! They have every advantage. They can disappear into the safety and comfort of the earth at the drop of a hat.

The ground hog, often called woodchuck, does one of the best disappearing acts. Too fat and clumsy to run fast, it digs a shaft that slants slightly downward into the ground. It sits and smiles on top of the open shaft, but no animal is quick enough to catch it. *Poof!* It vanishes, as through a trap door, into its runway deep underground.

In the spring, a lawn or a damp hillside meadow is plowed up by moles. These blind animals, with blunt snouts for driving ahead into the soil, can tunnel at the rate of fifteen feet an hour through millipede-sowbug territory. Every few feet, the mole pushes out the earth in a little mound, and the course of the shallow tunnel can be seen by the mounds. After the mole has feasted its fill on the millipedes and sowbugs, it retreats into a deeper tunnel and goes to sleep. This is why people hardly ever see moles. Jumping on their mounds to scare them out of the ground does no good. They are sound asleep in complete safety and comfort, deeper down.

So the solid ground is not so solid. It is a honeycomb of holes, large and small. It is full of life in every part.

The arch-enemy of the prairie dog is a black-footed ferret on the hunt. His long slim body can easily slip into prairie-dog's network of burrows.

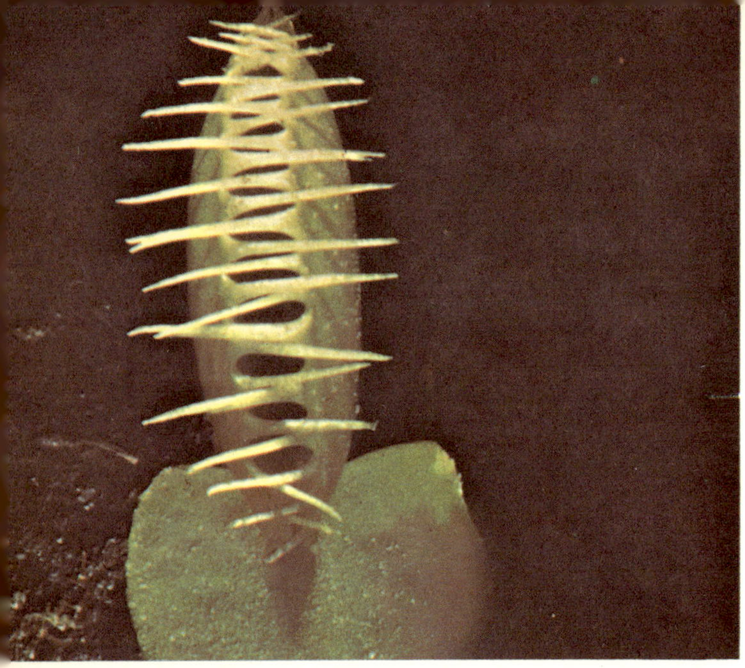

PLANTS THAT CATCH INSECTS

Although insects are strong, smart, and fast—while plants are rooted to the ground and unable to move—there are a few wonderful plants that catch and eat insects!

One of the queerest is the cobra plant, which has the shape and coloring of a hooded yellow snake with its head up, just on the point of making a final spring on its prey. However, instead of leaping to catch the insects, the plant invites them to catch themselves. From the top of the ramp, the insects fall into a "pitcher" of water and are drowned. Then the pitcher acts like a stomach that digests the prey.

The Venus flytrap works like a steel trap. Its leaves are hinged in the middle and open wide, like a book that has been laid open on the table. The leaves, pink, red, or green, and attractive on top, have the lure of flowers. Insects land on them and walk around looking for the nectar. But there are three little triggers on each half leaf, and when the victim stumbles over these the open "book" is slammed closed. As it comes together, long spines on the edges of the leaves fold over and enclose the prey behind prison bars so it can't escape. Then it is pressed and digested.

Another insect-eating plant looks like a bright jewel. It is called sundew because it sparkles so brightly. As it lies there it looks innocent enough. But little insects beware! The sparkle

Venus flytrap closes suddenly on its prey.

comes from sticky drops. If an insect lands on this brilliant plant, it will be caught like a fly on flypaper. The sundew also has tentacles, which fold over and seize the insect when it is struggling to get free from the stickiness. Held in what looks like a clenched fist, the insect is finally digested.

Nature, which never runs out of astonishing tricks, has also created a plant that catches for its dinner little animals which swim in ponds. The bladderwort works like a lobster pot. The trap is suspended, just below the surface of a pond, from floating leaves that look like spokes of wheels. Each trap has a hole at one end, with little fingers that swing in. A tiny swimming insect or fish will hit the trigger that is held out in front of the trap, and this opens the door. A current set up by the opening door carries the victim into the trap. The door closes behind, and no amount of pushing will make it open out. This is how a little animal comes to find itself inside the stomach of the dangerous but marvelous bladderwort.

Pitcher plant turns leaves into pitchers to drown its prey in deep wells of water.

SEEDS BY THE BILLIONS

Many millions of years ago there were only a few kinds of plants on earth fighting for a place in the sunlight. It was much easier than it is today for seeds to find places to grow. Then, simple seeds traveling by air and water kept plants spreading over the land. Trouble arose as, over millions of years, many new kinds of plants developed. Many plants then found themselves not on open hillsides, prairies, deserts, or other open areas, but in crowded jungles or thickets, and there was too much shade. The places where seeds could take hold easily were few and far between.

Where plants were much crowded, seeds that just fell and stayed there had a poor chance of growing. Seeds that were carried to other places by wind, water, or animals had a much better chance. Gradually, over millions of years, the plants that developed traveling seeds became much more common on the earth, while those that made stay-at-home seeds became fewer and fewer. Today we find that most

The ailanthus tree's seeds whirl through the air on wings curved like airplane propellers.

Seeds of the maple have stiff, rigid wings for gliding.

plants produce lots of seeds, and these seeds are scattered far and wide—as they must if only a few of them are to have a fair chance to grow.

Seeds take many, many forms. Seeds from poplars make "snowstorms" that whiten the ground. The parachutes of milkweed seeds look like a spilled load of cotton that has blown across the field. Often in mid-air you catch sight of little propellers whirling off the ailanthus and ash trees. The winged seeds of maple trees are long distance gliders.

Nature's great success with seeds is based on the law of averages. If it takes a thousand seeds to add one tree to the forest, that number of seeds will be produced many times over. To make a forest spread calls for billions of seeds.

Production of seeds by trees is topped by the grasses and flowers. A single plant of red clover, only a few inches tall, will turn out five hundred seeds from which little copies of itself will grow. The weedy crabgrass goes after ownership of the surface of the earth by making ninety thousand seeds on a single plant. Pigweed gives the crabgrass strong competition by moving into your yard with a million seeds per plant.

The plant that produces the greatest number of copies of itself is not a weed but one of the most prized and valuable flowers in the world, the orchid. The output of a single orchid plant has been estimated at 3,770,000 seeds. This shows how the law of averages works in the turning out of seeds, because it is very difficult for orchids to find a place to grow. They will not grow just anywhere. Many orchids grow only high up in trees, and their seeds must find spots on limbs that are wet, where the bark is a little decayed. To find places to grow when there are so few places available, an orchid makes millions of seeds, as light as the finest powder. Then the slightest whisper of wind will be sure to carry many seeds up among the branches.

Compare these smallest seeds with the biggest. The coconut palm leans over sea beaches, lakes, or streams. All it has to do is drop its big round seed, which rolls down the beach or splashes into the water. The little copy of the

Bright butterflies, attracted to showy blossoms, often help pollinate flowers. They unroll a curled-up, hollow proboscis, to sip the wells of nectar.

The blackberry wraps its seed in delicious fruit—to be eaten and scattered by animals and birds.

tree is enclosed in a huge round ball of white coconut meat that is oily and enables the seed to float. The coconut may be carried thousands of miles by currents and tides before it is rolled up on the beach by the waves, or pushed over a river bank by high water. Every seed of the coconut tree has such a good chance of success that a coconut palm does not have to produce its big seeds by the millions.

Not only do seeds stock the earth with plant life, but also there are many seeds left to provide fine food for animals. The extra seeds supply grains, berries, fruits, and such vegetables as peas, beans, and corn. Seed nuggets, especially berries, are the principal food of birds. A meadow mouse, weighing only a few ounces, loves seeds.

After the meadow mouse has eaten seeds and grass to make its body grow, it, in turn, is eaten by the cat, lynx, skunk, weasel, marten, mink, opossum, dog, fox, coyote, wolf, badger, bear, hawk, owl, eagle, crow, jay, magpie, sea gull, snake, or turtle—among others! The amazing multiplication of the tiny copies of plants in seeds is one of the most important secrets of living things.

Even on the gentlest currents of air, the seed of the milkweed floats by on parachutes of silky thread.

A DEAL WITH INSECTS

A grain of pollen is so small that it is invisible to the naked eye. Yet this tiny structure is a sort of blueprint of all the characteristics of the parent plant.

Up to the time it makes pollen an oak tree, for example, takes care of all its own needs as it grows in trunk, leaf, and flower. But when the pollen is ready to be joined with the ovule, or egg, of a female tree to form the seed from which a new individual will grow, the tree needs outside help.

Plants that do not have brightly colored flowers must depend on the wind to carry their pollen. They grow close together in open spaces. In this group are the grasses, including corn and wheat, and trees such as pine, oak, and birch, which have stood close together in breezy forests, and sycamore, elm, and willow, which pick up breezes coming through a valley or across water. Such plants simply release clouds of dry pollen into the air, and some of it is sure to hit targets all around.

But what about the plants with showy flowers? These grow in places sheltered from wind, or in thickets where there are lots of insects. These plants make deals with the creepers, walkers, runners, and fliers for carrying their pollen. The insects feed on the nectar of flow-

The silky threads on the seeds catch on the stiff pod of the milkweed, and their parachutes are pulled open.

Dragonflies, searching for small insects, often help pollinate the seeds of flowers.

ers, or carry it away to make food, as bees do. Some of the pollen, which is sticky, clings to their faces, bodies, and legs. So, as the insects travel from flower to flower, the pollen does too.

The showy flowers of these plants are vivid banners, like advertising signs on the front of a store, announcing that this is the place to pick up sticky pollen. The banners catch our eye and appeal to our nose, although it was not for us that flowers were invented.

The deal between plants and insects has given us the goodness of wild flowers and garden flowers, fruit trees and berry bushes, clovers, beans and peas and other vegetables, water lilies, and flowering trees such as magnolia, acacia, catalpa, and locust. The deal is very odd indeed. Neither side planned it that way; flowers and insects just grew up together. They have kept on helping each other because the deal works for both—and because they have no other way.

FLOWERS THAT DODGE THE RAIN

To keep their pollen powder dry, flowers build special structures, and twist and turn in the rain. Queen Anne's lace, for example, spreads a horizontal table of white flowers when the sun is out. If rain threatens at the time when the pollen of those flowers is ripening, the table tips to a vertical position, like round tables you stand against a wall. This happens when the stem, a couple of inches below the flowers, suddenly bends because of the dampness. It bends just enough for the weight of the flowers to make them sag to a vertical position.

Look across the pasture on a rainy day. Not all the Queen Anne's laces are tipped over. Older heads which have shed their pollen remain horizontal. Rain cannot hurt them.

Wild geraniums, buttercups, and many other field flowers act the same way. They droop in the rain only if the blossoms are young and contain fresh pollen.

Other field flowers such as dandelions, hawkweeds, and chicory close up on rainy days and at night to protect their pollen from rain and dew. Crocuses and pond lilies seem almost to vanish in the rain; they close up until the rain has stopped.

Flowers have great skill in keeping pollen dry. But when it comes to calling insects to help carry the pollen around, flowers seem almost human.

While gathering nectar from the thistle's flower, the monarch butterfly may dust it with pollen from a neighboring thistle.

Pollen clings to a bee's hairy body just as dust clings to a shaggy mop. When a bee enters a flower, it splashes about, gathering quantities of the yellow powder.

TO STING IS TO DIE

Everybody recognizes a bee and likes to see it capering among the flowers. It stands out in a crowd of insects because it is bigger than most, and makes a louder buzz, and never stops working.

Most people, when they think of bees, think about being stung. A bee's stinger is a spear that is pushed out from the bee's rear. It has nine barbs on each side, and is split down the middle so that the two halves slide back and forth on each other. This double spear is in a sheath that clasps it tight and works it by a strong muscle, which makes the two halves slide back and forth with a pumping action. After the spear enters the flesh, the barbs keep it from being withdrawn, and the instrument is driven farther in by pumping.

Bees sting only when afraid or mad. And when the worker honey bee stings a human being or a fleshy animal, the bee dies. Its barbs make the spear stick fast when it is driven in, and in trying to pull away from its own stinger, the bee tears its body fatally.

THE BEE FLYING MACHINE

A bee is built to carry heavy freight. It has storage space and lifting power to transport sirup, pollen, and varnish. All other flyers—birds, bats, and other insects—transport only themselves through the air, except for some light air mail, such as twigs and worms, which birds carry in their mouths.

Man's freight planes can carry a payload of only about 25 per cent of their weight, while a bee can carry almost 100 per cent. Man's plane has enormous, long, rigid wings for lifting and gliding, but they do not give it power to move forward. They can lift the plane only when it is going fast enough to create a strong suction above the wings. But the bee, with its very short wings on a big fat body, does not have to move forward to make its wings lift it. It needs no propeller or jet, because the wings both lift and drive this flying machine. It cannot glide, but it can move straight up or down, or hold still in mid-air.

The short, wide wings of this marvelous flying machine beat at high speed with a weaving figure-8 motion. By changing the shape of the 8, the bee is able to move forward, back, up, or down. With its amazing flying equipment, it can even hover in front of a flower.

The stubby wings of the bee fold in a split second when it dives into a flower or into tightly fitting cells of the beehive. It could not

Brilliantly colored flowers spread banquets of nectar and pollen for roving bees.

do the things it does if it had long, rigid wings like a dragonfly's. A dragonfly never folds its wings, but it never dives into flowers; it just perches on them.

The bee has two pairs of wings, very close together. For flying, these are joined by a row of hooks on the forward edge of the rear wings fastening into a pleat on the edge of the front wings. When wings are hooked together, they increase the wingspread of the bee. They can quickly be unhooked and folded together like a fan. The bee can also unhook the wings when it

wants to whirl them, to cool the beehive.

As a freight carrier the bee has three places for storing cargo. One is a tank inside its body, which it fills by sucking up nectar from the inside of the flower's body through a long tube. The other two storage places are "baskets" on its hind legs for carrying pollen and varnish. Imagine a freight plane with its load dangling underneath on the landing gear! But this method has worked well for a long time. Man first wrote about the bee in 3000 B.C., and the bee hasn't changed since.

After spending the night in the hive, bees start out in the morning empty. Outward bound, each bee takes on only a speck of honey for fuel, enough to reach the flower goal, where it knows it can refuel for the return trip. There is so much power in honey that a bit of it the size of a pinhead will carry the bee a quarter of a mile.

If nectar in flowers is flowing strong and anthers are bursting with pollen, the bee can suck up a load of sirup in a minute. It can build up two big, bulging loads of pollen in the baskets on its hind legs in three minutes.

A bee may carry water in its honey tank if the hive is thirsty. It may scrape resin off sticky buds and twigs, especially from poplar, horse-chestnut, willow, and honeysuckle buds, and load this into the outside carriers. This resin will be made into varnish to coat tree hollows and to stop up cracks and crevices in the hive.

When it is loaded up, a bee flies straight home, with a tankful of nectar inside and two bags of pollen swinging below—helping to keep the flying machine on an even keel. A loaded bee cannot fly upside down. It is not an acrobat like the housefly.

LOADING THE POLLEN BASKETS

Packing big loads of pollen on the outside of the hind legs, at the places called the pollen baskets, would seem almost impossible without a well-trained ground crew. The job is not merely a matter of scooping up pollen grains and tossing them into the pollen baskets the way you toss apples into bushel baskets. To keep the pollen from blowing away or falling off in mid-air, the loads must be moistened, pressed together like a snowball, molded, tamped down, and evenly balanced on each leg. Moreover, the pollen is collected from not just one, but many, flowers. Yet, a bee is so quick and efficient that it can collect and make up its

Pollen drops from the swaying corn tassels onto the sticky cornsilk below.

pollen loads in three minutes—a wonderful example of animal skill.

To collect pollen, a bee dives into a flower, scrambles around, rolls over, acts like a boy playing in the surf. The splashing throws pollen grains all over the body, where it sticks to little feathered hairs. When the bee is diving for nectar, its body picks up pollen by brushing past the pollen boxes, which are usually held out in front of the flower on long stems.

The bee leaves the flower and, while hovering at a point in mid-air, or perhaps while swinging below the flower and hanging on by one claw, it combs off its face, the top of its head, the back of its neck, with its front legs. Even the bee's eyes collect pollen, for hairs grow out of its eyes. The bee has a special soft brush to remove this pollen.

A reverse gulp brings up a speck of honey from the tank. This moistens the pollen. The middle legs scrape off the middle of the body, reaching way up over the back. A rapid sequence of combings and passings gets the wetted pollen onto the hind legs, where the scrapings are caught in a wide comb with nine rows of bristles. Then the bee doubles up its legs, while a row of bristles on them combs the pollen out of the nine rows of bristles. This operation deposits the pollen in the baskets, where it is pressed by the knee joints. When the bee bends its knees, the jaws of the press open; when it straightens its legs, the jaws close and the pollen is pressed and pushed up into the pollen basket.

The pollen basket is a shallow trough in the middle of the leg where it is wide like the blade of a paddle. To hold the load, there are curving hairs around the edges that serve the same purpose as stakes around a wagon bed. In the center of the basket is a single rigid hair. This makes it possible to build twice as big a load. As the pollen ball grows bigger and bigger, the hairs that embrace it are pushed apart and the load mounts above them. The long rigid hair gives the load a core. It holds the big ball together like a pole in the middle of a haystack.

BEE SCOUTS

All this skill and equipment is useless unless the bee can get to the right place at the right time. Bees do not camp out all night among the flowers. They go home and wait in the darkness of the hive until sunrise. There is no telling which flowers will be opening their pollen boxes and gushing nectar the following morning—or where those flowers are located. Different flowers bloom in different places every day.

When the hive stirs and greets the new day,

The bee sucks up nectar through a tube, and stores it in a tank inside its body.

there are about ten thousand little flying freight cars ready to go out and load up. They will not start, however, until they are told where they are going—the exact direction and the distance.

The queen is not the one to do it; the queen never issues an order. She is entirely occupied with laying eggs, and knows nothing about flowers, their pollen, and nectar. She might go out into the sunlight only twice in her life.

At sunrise a few bees, maybe a dozen, set forth in different directions to scout around the countryside to see what the new day offers in the way of ripe flowers. Several of the scouts fly around in the vicinity of the hive in ever-widening circles. If there is an apple orchard, a field of poppies, alfalfa, or a garden of peas or beans close by, great will be the excitement in the hive, and the whole army will be on the wing in a few minutes.

But the day's best plunder may be some distance away, and some of the scouts will have to search across miles of countryside. When one of these returns with glad tidings, it will tell the others exactly what kind of flowers are open, give them a compass bearing for the direction, and announce the distance to the spot.

Each thread of silk channels a grain of fertilizing pollen to a single kernel in the ear. Once the pollen grain reaches its destination, the seed begins to ripen.

Nurse bees are kept busy feeding the grubs of baby bees.

BEE TALK

This sounds like Alice's Wonderland, where animals act like people. The fact is that bees can talk to each other.

Birds utter singing commercials when they are hungry or in love. Ants blaze trails with odors to guide other ants. Porpoises call their families around them with childlike squeals and shouts. Elephants trumpet, lions roar, dogs bark, cats meow, bullfrogs croak, katydids katydid, swans whistle, mice squeak, cows moo, and roosters crow. But all of these communications of the animal world merely tell how the animals feel. The honey bee, however, speaks a language which gives a lot of information and some good advice.

A worker bee rams pollen into a storage cell, driving it home and packing it tightly with his head.

When the bee scout finds treasure, it fills its tank, packs its baskets, and makes a beeline to the hive. There other bees crowd around while the scout announces its findings. If it does this with a weaving dance, turning to the left and then to the right, it is saying: "Plenty all around! Go and get it!" The bees crowd up excitedly, touch the dancer with their antennae to pick up the odor—so as to know the right kind of flower to look for— and then fly off. But if the treasure is at some distance from the hive, and is perhaps a single tree or small patch of flowers, that would be like finding a pinprick on the map, and the searchers would get lost if they didn't have exact information. In this case, the scout, instead of weaving around, runs in a straight line, wagging its rear. At the end of the line,

A bee returns to the hive, the baskets on its rear legs bulging with heavy loads of pollen.

which is only an inch or so long because there isn't much space cleared in the big crowd, it turns to the left and circles back to the starting point. Then it runs straight forward again along the same line, circles to the right—and repeat! (All the time wagging vigorously.)

The straight-line run points directly at the flowers. The speed with which the speaker circles left and right tells the distance. The farther off the flowers are, the slower the bee circles back to the starting point. For example, if it makes ten circles in fifteen seconds, the flowers are three hundred feet away. But if it moves in slow motion, say two circles in fifteen seconds, the flowers are almost four miles away!

The amount of honey or pollen is told by the wagging. If the wag is vigorous, the supply is abundant—everybody should go and get it. If the wag is lazy, there's only a little, just a few should go, while the others wait for another scout to arrive from another area.

This marvelous way by which bees talk to each other was discovered by a patient scientist named Karl von Frisch. He spent many years trying to translate bee language.

THE MARBLE PALACE

This furry little ball of life with its great flying power, its weird equipment for plundering flowers, its big eyes for seeing where it is going (two bulges with 6,300 eyes in each bulge occupy most of its face), and its ability to talk to other bees about flowers, does not have a life of its own.

The honey bee is an animal of sunshine and fresh air, and its buzz is the song of a summer day. It fits so beautifully into our world, and

This honeybee rapidly fans its wings to drive moisture off nectar, which is to become honey.

The large queen bee is surrounded by attendants who constantly feed her royal jelly.

does such a fine job of sparking the seeds of flowers, that we can hardly believe what a different world bees live in—the strange world of the hive. Unlike other animals, a bee does not have babies and raise its own family; it does not build its own home, eat its own food, or fight its own battles. It lives for the hive.

The hive is a very beautiful building. It has rows and rows of six-sided rooms built with pure waxy walls that look like marble. Around this building clusters a dense throng of bees. A small hive has twenty thousand; a middle-sized hive fifty thousand or seventy-five thousand; and a big hive two hundred thousand.

The hive is not a city of many families; it is just one big family. One extra-large bee, the queen, lives in the heart of the hive, and she alone has produced these thousands. The queen works hard to lay up to two or three thousand eggs per day. But before we speak more of her, let's see what strange magic builds the white bee building.

Man takes raw materials and changes them into building materials such as steel, glass, rayon, and plastic. Some animals, too, change raw materials for building. Wasps chew up wood and spread the mash on the nest; the mash turns into gray paper when it dries. Termites also chew wood and, mixing the wood with soil, they make cement towers taller than a man and so hard that a pickax is needed to break them. Caterpillars and spiders squeeze out silk threads, made out of their ordinary food of leaves or insects, and spin fanciful living quarters that are delicate and swing with the wind. The honey bee pulls out of its vest pocket a fine building material for its marble palace, and puts this together by pushing, molding, and patting.

The marble palace, or comb, is built by young bees, those under seventeen days old, who have not reached the stage of flying off to fill their honey tanks and pollen baskets. The bees will hang themselves up in festoons from the roof of the hive or the hollow of a tree. One hooks its claws to the roof and another hooks onto the hind legs that dangle down. As more and more bees hook their front legs to the hind legs of those above, the chains grow longer. As they sway and touch, bees hook on to each other right and left, also, forming a living curtain. Nobody knows why they hang up in this way to produce wax, but it's a good guess that wax comes faster when the body is stretched out.

On each side of a bee's abdomen are four wax pockets. After about twenty-four hours of hanging, slips of wax appear out of these pockets, resembling tiny letters. When a bee feels that its wax is ready to come all the way out, it climbs up over the other bees, takes the wax letters out of its pockets, chews them, and pats on the wax where the comb is to be built.

Sometimes the wax scales come out fast, especially if a great many bees have hung themselves up at about the same time, and then wax scales litter the floor. This extra supply of wax for the bees is like a load of lumber dumped near their job for workmen. The lowest bees on the curtain let go of the legs of the ones above, drop to the floor, pick up the slabs, and buzz with them over to where the white walls are rising.

ROWS OF SIX-SIDED ROOMS

Honey bees seem to take pride in being good architects and engineers. They build rows and rows of little rooms all the same size, each one six-sided, with three pairs of walls facing each other. This beautiful structure takes shape under the feet of little six-legged creatures that run around and work like mad. They do not have drawing boards and compasses and rulers, but the job is well measured, balanced, and strongly put together.

The wax used in the walls is reinforced by drawing long thin threads of varnish through it while it is soft. As the wax hardens around these threads, the walls of the bee's hive are strengthened like concrete reinforced with wires. Varnish is used also to coat rough places in the tree hollow which the bees brush against in going and coming.

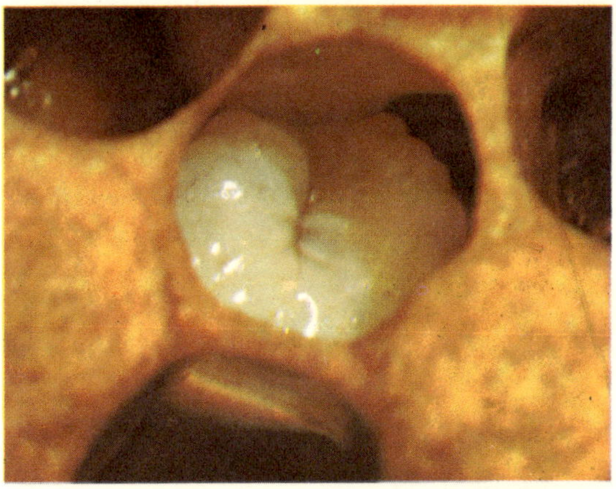

(a)

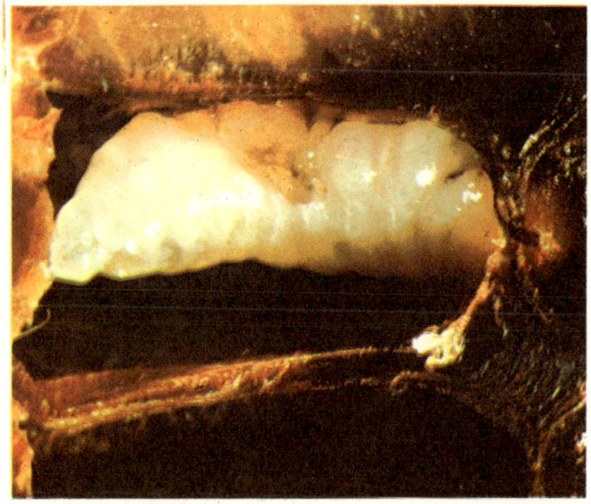

(b)

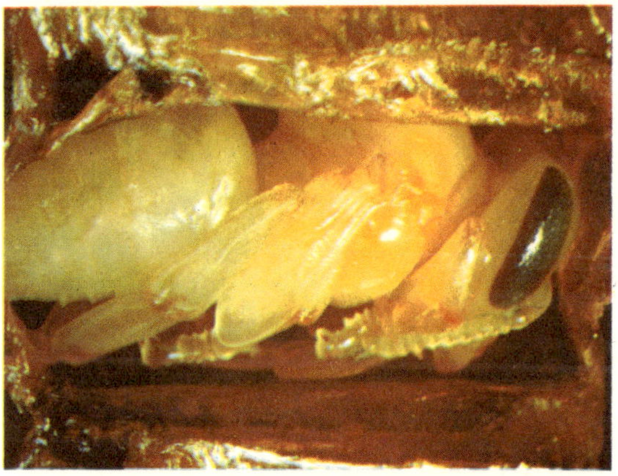

(c)

(d)

Fed by nurse bees, the grub (a) spins itself into a cocoon (b), develops into the pupal stage (c), and finally emerges (d) as an adult worker.

The bee scrambles about in the flower, collecting pollen everywhere on its feathered hairs.

The walls of the cells are very thin, only 1/350th of an inch! You couldn't even see a thread so fine, but this would be a sharp edge to a bee's tiny feet, and since bees spend most of their time running around on top of their comb, the top edges must be thickened. So extra wax is dabbed on and the tops of the walls are given a rounded coping. This makes the outside of the whole building like a screen that is comfortable to run around on.

Bees begin building a hive by just piling on wax. It is laid on like mud, as when a swallow builds a nest. The holes begin as rough cups, pressed in by the bee's body, and the cells will always be that size and exactly fit a bee. The work of shaping and finishing the cells is done by many bees in many holes, all pushing against each other. They use heads, feet, bodies—scraping, smoothing, and ramming home the wax, which is kept warm by the high temperature of their hard-working bodies.

The secret of the bee's skill lies in the way it uses natural forces. Any soft stuff like putty, clay, or warm wax will become thin as you push against it from opposite sides. If the cells of a comb are all pushed at the same time against each other, their walls will become six-sided, just as in a group of soap bubbles. That is a shape which makes them cling close together without spaces between. This wonderful law of nature is what makes the fine architecture of bee combs. The bees just make rough cups, then get into them, and push!

BUSIEST ANIMALS ON EARTH

The cells are used to raise babies and as storage tanks for honey and pollen. The tanks when full are capped with a neat little lid of wax. In winter, when food is scarce, the cap is torn off and honey or pollen, whatever the tank holds, is used by all the bees. The bee which takes out the honey passes it around.

To prove that a bee never digests its own food, but that the whole hive eats the same food and all digest it together, some scientists fed six bees in a hive of 24,500 bees honey that was radioactive. After two days, all bees in the hive were radioactive.

Most bees are busy collecting from the flowers, building their wax home, storing up honey and pollen, and passing around food. A few extra-big bees—the drones, or male bees—never do anything. They don't even take the trouble to reach into a tank of honey or pollen for food. They ask the other bees who are pass-

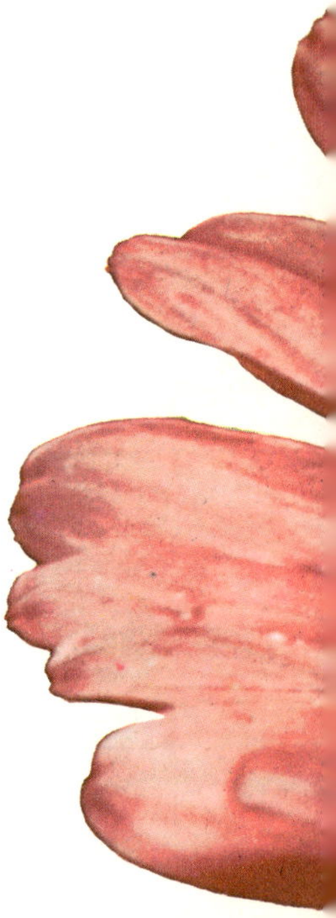

This bee scout will tell the workers in the hive what kind of nectar it has discovered, and how to find more of it for themselves.

ing food around to give them some. The drones are waiting for a chance to fly off into the sky just once, chasing after the queen. That is all the drone bee does in its life. It has no pollen baskets, but it does have bigger wings and flying power and bigger eyes to pursue the queen when she is a fast-flying speck in the air.

THE AMAZING QUEEN MOTHER

There is only one queen in the hive. Like the drones, she never does any collecting from flowers, building with wax, and passing around food. But she is not lazy. She is as important to the hive as a heart is to an animal. A hive of fifty thousand to two hundred thousand bees must have that one queen in order to live.

To keep up the bee population, as many as several thousand babies must be born every day. That is the queen's job. She spends most of her time walking across the face of the comb, pausing briefly at each open cell to drop in an egg. In a single day she can lay two thousand eggs—an amount four times heavier than her own body.

How can this be? We find the answer in the mysterious power of a food called royal jelly. This food, which looks like a sticky cream, can be made only in the head of a young bee. Moreover, a bee must be a certain age to make royal jelly—six to twelve days old. During that week, it chews pollen that it has taken out of the tank in the comb and mixes this with a peculiar kind of saliva. The result is royal jelly.

(a)

(b)

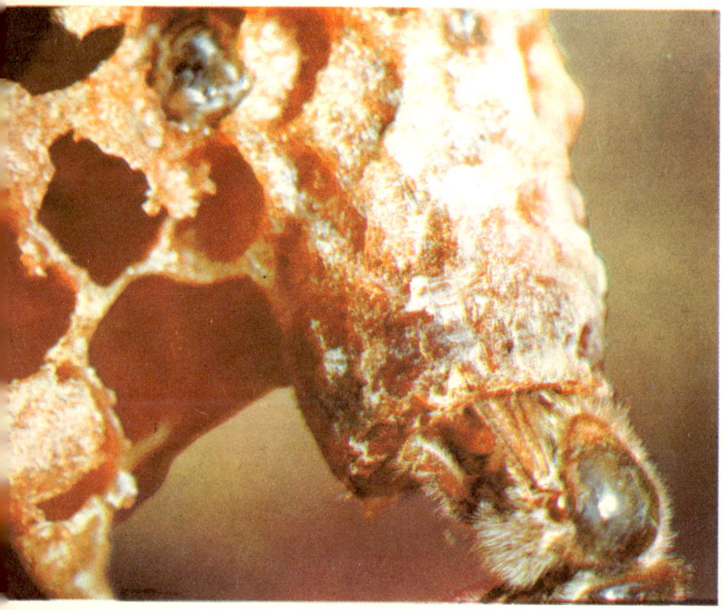

(c)

Queen bee grub, surrounded with royal jelly, is packed into a peanut-shaped cell (a) and tended by workers (b) until the adult queen (c) emerges.

When the queen is laying eggs, she is surrounded by some twenty bees making royal jelly. They face toward her and surround her like spokes of a wheel. Their entire job is to keep feeding her royal jelly. Every day about three of them pass the twelve-day-old mark and have to be replaced by younger bees, probably six-day-olds.

Wherever the queen turns while she is egg laying, the group of royal jelly feeders also turn. Wherever she goes, they go. About every twenty minutes she stops, and one of the jelly feeders steps up and pumps her full of the royal jelly which makes her lay more eggs. This meal takes about three minutes. The chief ingredient of royal jelly is pollen; so, in a sense, the dust that sparks the seeds of plants is being turned into bee eggs.

The queen is a special invention. Other bees work so hard all their lives that they don't have time to have children. To keep bees living on earth, nature invented the queen, who is different from all the others and able to produce all the children. She is not allowed to do any other work.

The queen has a pair of fine wings, but she uses them on only one or two occasions in her long life. One of these is her flight from her hive with a swarm, to start another hive.

If a queen dies by accident, or she isn't laying enough eggs, the bees get excited and set about making a new queen as fast as they can. First, they build an extra-big cell, roughly dabbed together in a hurry. This special queen cell, the shape of a peanut, hangs from the outside of the comb. The bees put an egg from one of the regular cells into the queen cell. Sometimes they take a baby bee already hatched. If the baby isn't over three days old, it is not too late to turn it into a queen. This baby is fed all the royal jelly it can eat.

Starting with a fresh-laid egg, it takes fifteen days to produce a queen in this way. But if the

Bees hang in chains, making wax for their hives. As they stretch themselves, thin slips of wax begin to emerge from their abdominal plates.

bees start with a one-day-old baby, they can create a queen in eleven days. The grown-up queen stands around getting her bearings and stretching her wings for three days. The bees keep feeding her royal jelly, but she can lay no eggs until after the mating flight.

Meanwhile the drones have bestirred themselves for the first time in their lives. They prance around the entrance of the hive, clean their antennae carefully again and again, and clean their big eyes (the drones have 13,090 little eyes in each eye—more than twice as many as ordinary bees have). If the weather is fair, around four o'clock in the afternoon of the fourth day after she grew up, the queen dashes off into the sky, with the drones after her. When she returns to the hive a half hour later, she is ready to lay eggs for the rest of her life.

BATTLE TO THE DEATH

The only thing that makes a queen assert herself is to have another queen around. She seems overcome with fierce jealousy. This happens when a fresh queen has been produced while the old queen is still in the hive. Then the two queens fight it out to the death.

The stinger of a queen is long and curved, and has no barbs. The queen can pull it out without killing herself. She can stab her enemy again and again. A duel between two queens is a terrible battle to the death, with each trying to drive home the poisoned spear first. The other bees instinctively know that a hive can have but one egg-layer, and so they urge on the fighting bees. If one turns away for a second, the others push her back to the attack. Fighting queens are not allowed to stop until one is killed.

Two queen bees, piping shrilly, battle fiercely to the death.

The fearless black ant (left) prepares to attack a huge velvet ant.

A queen may sound a high, clear note as a battle cry called "piping." Perhaps it results from her breathing hard in excitement. Like the notes of a flute, it is made when she forces air through ten little holes in the side of her body.

THE SWARM

Sometimes the older queen does not fight it out with the young queen. Finding out that another queen is being brought up in her hive, she prepares to leave the place without delay and take along a good part of the population.

There is great excitement in the hive when a swarm is being made up to leave. Bees may neglect to go out and gather nectar. Their whole routine is upset.

A swarm is a terrifying flying ball consisting of thousands of bees. A big swarm may have as many as thirty-five thousand bees, but ordinary swarms have five or ten thousand. All are workers, with one queen in their midst, moving out to find a place to build a new hive. This is the second time that the queen bee uses her wings.

The buzzing ball shoots up out of the hive, swirls around crazily, and then heads in one direction. After buzzing around for a while,

the swarm comes to rest on a limb of a tree or any firm place it happens to touch. Then it waits for scouts to bring back news of a good hollow in a tree, or a protected place in which to build a comb. When that news comes, the swarm is off again to the new location. There it hangs up its living curtain, and bees start taking wax letters out of their vest pockets.

So bee life goes buzzing along.

THREE BUGS IN A ROW

An ant looks like three tiny bugs fastened together in a row on a piece of pipe. The one in front is the head; the middle one is the chest, or thorax; the one on the rear end, the abdomen, is the biggest of all.

If the ant is broken apart, each segment can go on living separately for a little while. Each has its own supply of blood, its own breathing tubes, its own openings into the outer air closed by its own valves, and separate nerves to operate the muscles. Even after the head is cut off, the jaws can go on biting, the feelers feeling. The middle part, with its six legs, can go on running and kicking. The rear part can go on doing what it was just doing—whether laying eggs, stabbing with a stinger, or performing as a bottle of honey.

There are more ants than any other kind of dry-land animal in the world. Ants are so successful because they can live almost anywhere. A handful of soil makes a home; or a bit of rotten wood in a tree or a fallen log will do. Or cracks in your house or barn. Ants are not particular.

Bees eat only pollen and nectar; so if there are no flowers around, there can be no bees. But ants eat all sorts of things. Their chief food is dead insects, no matter what kind, and these are plentiful. One man who spent a morning counting dead insects being lugged and pushed into an ant nest figured that 13,500 bodies would be handled during one eight-hour day.

An apple or any other fruit that is bruised by falling to the ground is luscious to ants. Ants like food soft and squashy. They love seeds of grasses and berries, but wait for decay to soften them first. Some ants plant the seeds, and when these start to sprout, an ant bites off the root tip to keep it from growing, and there is a delicious fresh vegetable all ready to eat.

Ants pass up fresh pollen, which is crystal and hard, but they like sweet juices such as sap, or sweet stuff from bodies of other insects.

Ants will take the nectar of flowers if they can get it. But flowers reserve their nectar for bees. Flowers may have bristles that stop crawling ants like a barbed wire, or sticky places where crawling ants get stuck. Some plants have their flowers on vibrating, slippery stems, which shake the ant off before it can get to the flower.

A blind snake enters the ant hill and begins eating the white ant babies it discovers underground.

But ants do not starve for lack of nectar; they have a large menu to choose from.

GIANT STRENGTH

When an ant carries a fat, dead moth twenty-seven times as big as itself, through the grass, that calls for strength and skill. The ant cannot follow a path along the ground, because the stems would block the outstretched wings. It has to be up high, with more open space, where the moth can be tipped up or down, turned this way and that. This job compares to a man's carrying an airplane through a jungle.

The ant does not try to lift and carry, but drags, pushes, pulls, and upends the load. All the time it runs around from side to side, up in front or behind; it works like a demon, never pausing. It has six legs to brace against the grass while it nudges the load along with its head. It can even take a stand with three legs and use the others for supporting the load or as levers.

With long legs spread far apart, and body hung low, the ant is built for super-leverage, strong bracing, powerful dragging, pushing, pulling. It even uses its elbowed antennae for support at times. These keep up a rapid fire of taps on the moth's body and surrounding grass, sizing up the situation every instant. Somehow the moth keeps moving toward the place where the ant wants it.

This animal is like a team of eight workers. The first two, the feelers, or antennae, are out in front, sweeping a wide circle with lightning strokes. If smooth going lies ahead, they tap the surface like long legs running backward. Meanwhile, behind the feelers, the front legs are extended forward and operate with a pull-ing action like oars. The middle pair of legs

Nurse ants pick up the ant larvae and begin hurrying them to safety.

Soldier ants instantly attack the snake.

are wide-spread to cradle the whole body while they walk with rapid steps. Finally, the rear legs, extended far out behind, keep up a series of strong pushes. Two foremen, two pullers, two supporters and walkers, and two pushers— that's why an ant can carry such big loads.

During most of the trip through the jungle no other ants come out to help. But when the giant dinner gets near home, perhaps where they can smell the food, helpers come.

Ants may work alone or together. They can quickly and easily bring pebbles from their tunnels underground, even though, in proportion to their size, those are big boulders which a man would take a bulldozer to move. They not only can push rocks around to clear tunnels, but arrange them in circles around the entrances for protection.

THE MATING FLIGHT

Ants that are busy digging tunnels, hauling food, and running trails do not grow wings. Outstretched wings would soon be damaged or broken among grass stems, leaves, cracks, and tiny holes. But there comes a time when ants are developed that have wings. These are males and a few queens which are going to lay eggs. On a clear afternoon when there is little wind, these winged ants fly off on a mating trip into the sky. After some zooming through the sky, the males drop to the ground; they can't run and hide, because of their wings. They flop around until the birds get them.

The larvae are put down, out of danger, in another underground room.

A deadly enemy, the red ant, discovers the black ants' tunnel.

The queen ant also drops to the ground, but her wings can be easily torn off. She does this with her jaws and front feet. Then she digs a hole as fast as she can. Because a queen is not a tunnel digger, like other ants, this is hard work for her. Her jaws wear down, hairs are scraped off her body, her smooth polished armor gets scratched and bruised. But dig she must before a bird spots her.

When the hole is deep enough to hide in, she pulls a stone or some dirt over the top, snuggles down, and lies in there quietly for about three months, until her eggs hatch. After that, with children to do the digging, real tunneling can start and the family can grow.

Ants live long, compared to other insects. While a bee dies in six weeks, ants live for years. An undisturbed colony may grow a population of hundreds of thousands and build a vast system of tunnels and rooms.

The eggs keep hatching. Four months after the first ones hatch, a crowd of bigger and stronger tunnelers appears. Two years later the colony is so large that special guards are needed, and the eggs develop into soldier ants to take their places at the entrances. Three years after the lost queen dropped to the ground, some ants in the colony are developed that have wings, another flight goes off into the sky, and another queen drops to earth and starts digging furiously.

The red ant cuts the black sentry in two with his jaws. Soldiers from both armies join the struggle.

NO FEAR OF GIANTS

Ants are better protected against enemies than any other animals on earth. Even a keen-eyed bird has trouble picking up a target that disappears while you look at it.

But a small snake, called a worm snake, may glide through ant tunnels looking for the room where the ants' babies are hidden. When this happens, some of the ants carry their babies through the connecting galleries into rooms deeper underground. Others attack the monster without hesitation, and although they are pigmies in comparison, they put up a terrific fight. They kick with all their legs, and stab, cut, bite, and tear with their jaws.

A huge, strong beetle may be attacked and eaten by ants; so may a grasshopper. But some grasshoppers have eardrums down on their forelegs, and these can hear sounds of little insects in the grass. Some ants can wheel around and use the stingers on their rears like a fire hose. They can squirt invisible sprays of stinging poison as far as eighteen inches. To protect themselves from such pesky little ants, the

The desperate battle begins.

Parasol ants carry supplies of fresh green leaves to their underground gardens.

grasshoppers can only release the springs of their mighty hind legs and leap to safety in the air.

THE WARS OF THE ANTS

The most dangerous foes of ants are other ants. All the cruel weapons, the fierce strength of ants, all their skill in maneuvering, and their stabbing and poison equipment, are used mostly against other ants that raid their homes and carry off their children.

Ants are strong enough to carry pebbles many times their size.

Here is a big family of the familiar black ants going about their business—running tunnels, raising children, cleaning up dead insects in the vicinity, lugging in food. But one day an ugly stranger turns up and looks over the tunnel entrances. He knows there are hidden galleries at this place filled with white bundles which are the babies of black ants.

He is richly colored, brown-red tinged with purple. His jaws stick far out on each side like curved scimitars—not made for peaceful troweling of tunnels, but to slash and pierce the armor of other ants. He is a dread Amazon ant.

The blacks rush to plug their holes with stones and pellets of dirt. They scatter pebbles and waste so that it doesn't betray the locations of their entrances. Sometimes they close all entrances. Then they retire into the safety of their tunnels.

Away over the hill, red ants are seething with excitement. Their scouts, searching the countryside, have brought back news of a black ants' nest. The reds pour out of their tunnels and line up in regiments. Soon the column begins to follow the odor trail made by the scouts—over the hill, across the road, straight to the hidden home of the blacks.

Now the red ants break ranks and hurry to pull out the plugs from tunnel entrances. Perhaps they find the holes—so carefully concealed—by following the scent trails of the enemy.

Suddenly, all at once, the reds dive into the tunnels. There is pandemonium underground. The reds are invading the rooms of the blacks and snatching up their babies. The blacks are also snatching up their babies and carrying them from room to room, trying to find a safe place for them.

Presently both reds and blacks pour from the tunnels, their jaws full of white bundles. These

Mushroom cotton grows on leaves the ants have hung from the ceiling of the cave.

The stomach of the honey-cask ant is swollen with delicious stores of liquid honey-dew.

bundles, which look like eggs, are the babies, the larvae. The blacks run around wildly, looking for a place to put their bundles. The reds carrying the kidnaped babies from a single column and head straight for home.

Ants traveling in single file follow the odor or touch of the next one in front. They do not use their eyes to see where they are going. They never stop pattering along while the next one in front keeps going. If ants proceeding in single file are caught in a sudden storm which washes away the trail, and an ant in front trying to pick up the scent happens to pick up an ant at the rear, the column will form a circle going nowhere. In that case the marchers may circle round and round until they fall dead.

But after this raid, the blacks do not willingly let the reds march off with the stolen babies. They attack, and a terrible battle is joined. They slash with their scimitars, stab with their stingers, squirt their poison vapors, bite off heads and legs. Parts of ants left after the heads are cut off go right on fighting. The field of battle is littered with pieces of ants and with white bundles dropped in the confusion.

Because the blacks usually outnumber the reds, they will probably drive them off and save many of the children. They pick up the children and put them back in the nest, and life goes on.

But those reds which get away with babies carry them back to their nests to be brought up as red ants. When they grow up, these stolen ants will be slaves in the nest of the reds. They will work the same way and just as hard as they would for their own family.

Different kinds of ants make war in different ways. Careful scouting, a compact and orderly march, and dives into the black tunnels at the same time are ways of the red Amazons when raiding the blacks. Another ant, the red formica, is also a great raider of black ants. But instead of a column, red formicas form a waving front several feet or yards across and ripple along in open formation. The columns spread and search for the black ant nests.

ANT DAIRY FARMERS

The ant farmers are on the job in spring as soon as the first thaw comes. They keep cattle, raise crops, and bring in a harvest of seeds.

The dairy farmers put their cattle in the barn at night and protect them all day. The "cattle" are little green insects, called aphids, which cluster on leaves and stems, sucking the juice. This juice is excreted as a sweet sirup called honey dew. The ants lap this up and love it as much as bees love nectar. They even "milk" the aphids by stroking their backs!

A very savage insect called an aphis lion loves to eat aphids, so the ants build a barn to keep aphids in. This is made by weaving bits of grass into a tunnel closed at one end. Sometimes ants carry the aphids into their underground rooms and care for them like babies. Or ants may collect aphid eggs in the fall, keep them carefully over the winter, and put them

A replete feeds drops of honey to the workers in the ant hill.

out on leaves in the spring when they are ready to hatch.

ANT GARDENERS

Perhaps the most delicious and nourishing vegetable cultivated in any garden is grown by ants—not all ants, just a few special ones. This vegetable, rich in protein and sugar, is so nourishing that they give up eating insects and live entirely on the garden crop.

Since ants are underground dwellers, they chose a kind of plant that grows well in darkness. This is a type of mold that will grow where it is dark, damp, and cool. In the ant galleries, mushroom "cotton" makes thick, luxurious gardens. These resemble bath sponges, full of holes that let in plenty of fresh air and permit the ants to run in and out. When the mushroom sponge is touched by secret chemicals from the mouths of the ants, it produces little bubbles, like cabbages. The ants bite off these

Living casks of honey hang from the ceiling. Workers must lift them back into place if they fall, as they cannot move themselves.

Nature provides lush leaves and grasses for the creatures of the field.

vegetable bubbles and eat them. Also, the ants lay their eggs on the cottony threads, and when these hatch, the new ants are lying in a bed of delicious food. The babies eat the bed and grow fast.

THE PARADE OF PARASOL ANTS

The mushroom cotton must be planted on fresh green leaves treated by the special ant chemical. Ant gardeners must keep busy running out to trees and bushes, cutting round pieces out of the leaves, carrying these back one piece at a time, and piling them up for the mushroom cotton to grow on. The parade of ants holding round green bits of leaves high over their heads is a funny sight. This is why they are called parasol ants.

The file of ants going from the nest to the green leaves meets the returning file proudly carrying the parasols along the same trail. The patch cut from a leaf is large and heavy, perhaps ten times as heavy as the ant carrying it. Yet the ant somehow lifts it up, balances it high overhead, and runs along with the load—like a man running along with the entire wall of a room held overhead!

The trail is barely wide enough for the two columns to pass. They dodge around each other like people on the sidewalk. If there is a pebble or a drop of water in the center, the paths divide to go around it. Sometimes they collide, and the ants stop, seem to say "*Sorry!*" and go on.

Often mysterious strangers join the leaf-carrying parade. One is an insect that is not an ant. It has a thin body with a tall bright green projection similar to the parasols carried by the ants. This insect impostor is hiding in the parade so as not to be snapped up by a hungry bird. It may even smell like the ants.

The parade of the parasol ants has hitchhikers, too. Toward the end of the day little ants can be seen riding as passengers en route to the mushroom garden. As many as seven have been counted riding on one upraised parasol. But these little ants are not just out for a ride. They lick the leaves to clean them, and paint the freshly cut edges with a sticky fluid like varnish to seal in the sap and keep out the germs. When riding on the parasols, they are on their way to work.

Everywhere the little ants are busy cleaning, while the bigger ants are cutting out parasols and doing the carrying. The mushroom garden must be clean and pure. Dust must not spoil the delicate flavor of its vegetables, and bacteria weeds would quickly spoil the garden.

HONEY CASK ANTS

Indians digging in the ground in the dry Southwest struck what looked like little green grapes. As they dug deeper, they kept finding more little grapes, down to about six feet. The grapes were juicy and sweet—delightful. But how could grapes grow deep in dry, hard ground?

These were not really grapes. They were bottles of honey—bottles with feet that wiggled, with tiny bodies and heads attached to them, with feelers that waved around!

Primitive man made wine bottles and water jars out of the skins of animals. But the bottles of the honey ants are whole live animals. They are ants which drink all the honey that is brought to them until they are swollen up as

Spikes of blue lupine are heavy with pollen. The scent of its nectar travels on the wind.

Butterfly weed flutters its colorful blooms.

Wild yellow orchids beckon to hungry insects.

round as a ball, and after that they will give a drink of honey to any ant that asks for it.

This custom helps the family to solve a big problem. Honey ants live on honey, but honeydew is plentiful only during a few weeks of the year, when aphids are around to have their backs stroked, or when gall insects are producing honeydew on oak trees. Gall lumps are the nests of little insects which suck up sap and make sirup out of it. The sirup oozes out of the gall only during the night, so the honey ants are on hand to get it then. They are night workers, unlike the ants that live on the bodies of insects, those that cut wheels out of green leaves, and those that make war.

Ants which eat only honeydew would all die of starvation when aphids and galls are out of season unless they could store up the honey. Then ants themselves become honey bottles. A honey bottle ant is called a "replete," which means "filled up." In a big family of honey ants as many as three hundred will be filled up with honey sirup. From the time they start becoming repletes, they never run outside again. The other ants do all the collecting of honeydew.

An ant starts turning into a honey bottle when it is young, before the armor of its body has hardened. Then the honey stomach, in the rear, can stretch. The head and chest remain the same size, but as more and more ants bring the replete drinks of honey, the rear part swells and swells until it is round as a grape.

The replete hangs itself from the roof of the cavern, holding on with the claws of its front feet. Dangling there, it can only wave its legs in the air. It is too fat to run around any more. If it gets knocked off, the other ants, with all their strength and skill, lift it back up and hook it on to the ceiling again. Ants take good care of their honey bottles, and these may live for years, patiently hanging from the ceiling.

THE WOODPECKER

In the living chorus called forth by early morning sunlight, the clearest sound is the woodpecker's rat-tat-tat. Fresh sunlight is warming the tree bark; this is his signal to be about his business as an expert wood-driller.

This fellow has to walk up a tree on his hind legs (his forelegs are wings). He has no hands to hold a drill, nor arms to swing a pickax, yet make a hole he must—standing on the vertical surface with his nose about an inch away. Nature has given the woodpecker a body that makes all this work seem simple and effortless.

He has two clawed toes turned forward for climbing and holding, and another two toes—some woodpeckers have only one—turned backward for clutching rough bark, as you clutch tightly with an opposing thumb. When the head starts moving like a hammer driving a nail, the very stiff tail feathers are turned down to act as a prop. It's a well-balanced, secure drill-rig!

The closed beak is wedge shaped and somewhat blunted at the tip. It can strike hard blows that make the chips fly, or it can be vibrated like a mason's drill to bore deep round holes,

Parent blackbirds are kept busy finding seeds and insects for their hungry fledglings.

The young blackbird (right) is ready to begin the dangerous and important business of learning to fly.

probing for beetles or ants under the bark or inside the wood. This sort of work calls for a special beak that will not soon break off. The woodpecker's beak is no mere attachment but a bony extension of its skull that can never be loosened by pounding.

A drill-and-ice-pick beak does not make good pincers for catching insects. But the woodpecker has a tongue attached to a long spring that circles over the dome of its head. As this weird tongue springs out far beyond the beak, a gluey drop of saliva is deposited on its tip. To this the ant or beetle larva sticks, and it disappears into the woodpecker in a split second.

The song and the beautiful colors of the American goldfinch are well known in the eastern half of the United States.

THE HUMMINGBIRD

The hummingbird must solve an even harder problem than the woodpecker's. It must stop in mid-air with no firm place at all to stand on. A hummingbird hunts nectar and little insects in flowers, but it is too big to stand on petals as does a bee—even though it is the smallest bird made, only about 2½ inches from beak to tail. So the hummingbird must hover tirelessly in front of a flower while it plunges in its long, suction-tube beak. The tongue, without protruding may act as a pump for the beak, but its real work is to lick up nectar, pollen grains, and little insects and carry them to the beak.

A hummingbird is the most aerial bird on earth. Not only can it poise at a spot in mid-air, but also, by changing the pitch of its wings, it can back up, and then suddenly shoot forward at twenty-four miles an hour, almost faster than the eye can follow. Its greatest speed, when diving to protect its babies, is said to be over sixty miles per hour.

A hummingbird's feet are used only for landing gear; it never hops or walks on them. Merely to turn around on the perch or move half an inch to the side, it takes wing. When pumping babies full of delicious pollen-nectar-insect formula, the tube beak acts as a siphon instead of a vacuum cleaner. The hummingbird stands on the edge of the nest or else hovers above it. Hovering is easier for shifting one's position to feed one baby after another.

In the early dawn, the spider's miraculous suspension bridge sparkles with dew.

THE CHICKADEE

Most birds which nest or hunt around trees and bushes must enter the canopy of twigs by coasting in from the open air, or must glide to a perch on outer branches. The paths in such places are a twisting labyrinth that calls for unbelievable diving, somersaulting, sudden flying up at a steep angle, split-second turning—all everyday stunts for the chickadee. This bird has feathers molded around a bullet-shaped body. It has very short wings that flash out and then hug the body, and a short tail.

This madcap flyer can snap up a caterpillar from a limb while turning a somersault.

It takes a lot of energy to keep this busiest, fastest bird in a tree going. It is a ravenous eater. If you stop and listen to it, you can tell that its egg-laying time is not far off. In the early spring, some weeks before the eggs are laid, this bird says "phoebe" instead of "chickadee."

Waiting motionless in the center of her web (a), the spider feels the tug of the strands as a grasshopper (b) struggles to get free. Spinning more sticky strands about her prey (c), the spider stings the grasshopper and hangs him up (d), to die.

THE FABLE OF THE SPIDER AND THE GRASSHOPPER

Of all the wonderful events set going by the morning sun, none is more marvelous than the stunt of the orb-weaving spider. With no wings of its own, it has a way to capture things flying through the air. Even prey many times bigger than itself can make a giant feast for the little spider.

(a)

(b)

We marvel at our modern suspension bridges, which take a year or two to build. A spider engineer spans as great a space, in proportion to its size, with a superb suspension bridge in hours rather than years!

Here is a space of about three feet between the outer branches of two bushes, ideal especially if there are grass and weeds underneath on the ground and busy insects using the area for their traffic. A tiny spider down on the ground sizes up this situation in some mysterious way and decides to act.

She runs up the trunk of one of the bushes and out on the limb facing the other bush at the highest spot of attachment of the web. She makes sure that the wind is at her back. Then she lifts up her abdomen and presses out a silky thread, which rapidly grows longer until it waves in the wind while carried toward the opposite bush. As the silk thread continues to lengthen, the tip finally touches the branch over there and becomes entangled. The spider then pulls in the slack and fastens the near end. She now has a rope bridge on which she can run back and forth, laying a few more strands to make it extra strong, for it will be the main cable for her structure.

Next she drops to a lower branch, spinning as she goes. Then she mounts to the top cable, crosses over, and drops to a lower branch on the opposite side. The frame of the web is taking shape.

Now she travels around and across, spinning out strands of silk behind her. As she runs she pays out the strands from a foot held out as far as she can reach, so that it will not get entangled. The construction is always in balance. First on one side, then on the other, she proceeds to the midpoints of spaces to make a drop. She hauls in the lines to give them just the right tension.

When spokes are all in place, the spider proceeds to the hub, right in the center, and weaves a silky mattress on which to rest—upside down as long as there is no rain or mist. (Moisture such as dewdrops on the web makes it beautifully visible—but the spider can catch nothing with wet strands.) To outward appearances she is getting a well-earned rest and, sound asleep in the center, she doesn't even bother to look around.

The signal that something has been caught comes as a telegraphic jerk on the line. A violent tug might be a grasshopper. Out dashes the spider, and before you can count three the big catch is revolving, being wound up in a heavy silk straitjacket.

All the spokes and spiral strands of the web

(c)

(d)

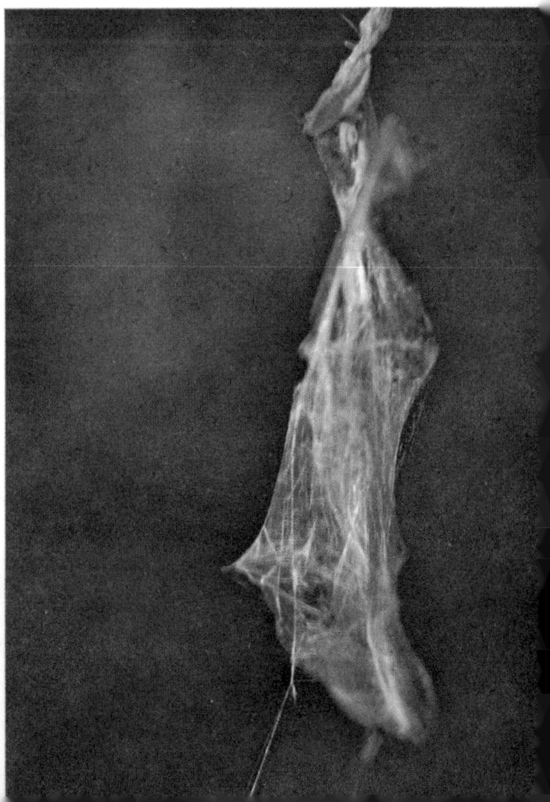

are sticky, the better to hold prey that strikes them, but the mattress where the spider lies at the hub is not sticky. Why doesn't she stick on her own web when she runs out across it? Because nature has oiled her feet so they will not stick. She wears overshoes!

THE CIRCUS IN THE FIELD

On a sunny summer morning, after a spell of dark weather, flowers open wide, golden pollen sparkles, colors are bright and vivid. Armies of odd little animals that have built up big appetites while waiting for the sun to shine suddenly appear. They have been hiding in the soil, under stones and leaves, or folded up in flowers. The bees among them have been heaving restlessly in the hive, making a deep buzz like a long-drawn-out snore.

To an insect a flower is tremendous. Goldenrod billows into the sky with the majesty of a thundercloud turned to gold. Queen Anne's lace holds high, on its long poles, acres of white landing stages. A lily is as big as a house, painted bright red or yellow, and as wide open as a bell. These enormous flowers are not just standing still. They dance up and down, quiver, flutter, and wave.

The cecropia moth caterpillar finds rich feasts at the end of every leafy green stem.

The sparkling colors, the delicious smells and the dancing in the breeze, announce the solemn fact that dinner is ready. The greatest feast in the world is provided in vast variety and quantity. Here are fruit juices, sap, nectar, pollen, and enormous side dishes of green leaves. There is plenty of food, all ready to be pounced upon and sucked up. Not one animal of the hungry hordes has to waste a lot of time digging or searching. It can chew, suck, and swallow as fast as it wants, and find more with a short hop or run or by merely turning its head.

Broad, smooth landing and standing platforms are laid out at every flower. At the lower ends of these, ramps lead straight down to bags of pollen or wells of nectar. If the footing is slippery or the ramp is very steep, nice soft hairs that feel good to the feet are used as a carpet. Flowers such as the iris or lily, that keep their nectar at the bottom of deep wells where only a long sucking tube can reach it, mark their targets with lines and spots or a black shadow in a white circle.

Insects, with all their excitement when going after flowers, are mostly as silent as sunlight. The buzz and whirr of bees, dragonflies, hawk moths, and grasshoppers are not emotional, but mechanical sounds like those of whistling jets and humming propellers. The click of a click beetle, when it leaps into the air after being laid on its back, is not a shout of joy, but the release of a spring. Ants also click sometimes, but nobody knows whether they are mad or having a friendly conversation.

If we had a sound microscope, we might hear a wonderful hubbub among the insects and flowers. This would include the tinkle of sap through stems, the tiny footsteps of tiny hordes, and the splash of a proboscis into a drop of nectar. But probably we would not hear any laughter or squeals of delight. It is serious business for those who invade the flowers.

But from our viewpoint there are amazing acrobatics, feats of diving, stunt flying, running and wriggling races. Aphids are clowns that tip over with great seriousness, do a handstand, get their "noses" caught, kick their legs in the air, but are unable to free the caught nose. Click beetles are clowns too. Touch one slightly and it drops as though shot. Landing on its back, it plays dead for a while and then suddenly gives a click and pops up into the air. If it comes down on its back again, it clicks and pops again, and keeps this up until it happens to land on its feet; then it runs off. All this takes place amidst flags flying and a wonderful rhythm of motion, with leaves waving and flowers bending and quivering.

All the time bees are making beelines to flowers, butterflies are fluttering around leisurely. They zigzag and turn in mid-air like blown leaves. The butterfly is not as hungry as other insects. Its other self, the caterpillar, has the huge appetite of this marvelous animal that leads a double life. A butterfly is more interested in a warm spot to stand on and stretch its wings. It will rest on a sun-warmed leaf as readily as on a flower. However, it likes an occasional drink of nectar, which it gets through a long tube as though it were sucking through a soda straw. The butterfly gets this nectar from flowers that have deep nectar wells. While it is on the wing, the butterfly carries its sucking straw coiled up like a watchspring under its chin.

From a caterpillar's viewpoint, flowers and leaves tower into the sky, with vast open spaces and chasms between them, and they shake violently. Yet what looks like an impossible feat of mountain climbing is accomplished easily by the caterpillar. To get around in the weird flower world it has eight feet on short legs that take a powerful grip. It can grab with two feet at one end and stretch out to bridge a gap. It hurries along with a rippling motion on a flat surface, and bends double turning around the edge of a petal or leaf.

The red flowers of the maple tree are among the miniature wonders of springtime.

The tiny pink and purple flowers of the pine may be seen only by sharp-eyed observers.

Colonies of barnacles cover the rocks on the shoreline like patches of winter snow.

THE MEASURING WORM BUFFOON

In the midst of all the commotion of whirring, fluttering, diving, and running, a little buffoon can be seen proceeding slowly across a leaf. It walks with half of itself always standing still. This is the measuring worm going places by absurdly looping up and flattening out. This is the only way it can walk, because its body is long, soft, and saggy and has no legs for support in the middle. The front end walks forward, stretching out. Then the front end stands still while the rear end walks up, causing the middle to rise in a tall loop.

In early summer when leaves are fresh green, the measuring worm is light green, but toward the end of the summer when things are turning brown the measuring worm turns brown too—dark brown, exactly the tone of a twig. Then this well-fed animal takes a mighty grip with its hind legs, stiffens, and stands out at a right angle. Its body even copies the humps and irregularities of a twig! The strength of that grip which permits a solid inch of caterpillar to stand out at a right angle can only be imagined when you try to grab a small tree trunk and hold yourself at arm's length horizontally for hours.

"WHITEWASH"

They look like splashes of whitewash on rocks and wharf piling when the tide goes out. They are as hard as rock and so strongly cemented that you can't scrape them off without crushing them.

We are talking about barnacles, of course.

A barnacle is a kind of shrimp which leads three lives. It is born under water as a little triangular animal called a "nauplius," with one eye, two pairs of legs, and one shell. The nauplius swims around with millions of other animals that rise toward the lighted ceiling by day and sink in the dark water by night.

A week or so after birth, the nauplius changes from a triangular creature that swims around freely into an oval animal compressed between two shells like a clam. This animal is called a "cypris." Unlike the clam, the cypris has six pairs of legs, on which it can walk at the rate of one inch per hour. When it is lifted on the high tide, it explores for a place to live. Finding a bare spot where the currents are not too strong, it puts its head down while it presses cement out of its feelers. It builds this cement into a pile around itself. After that it never takes another step. Nature has destined it to be a prisoner for the rest of its life.

This weird animal may live for years between the tides, most of the time under water, part of the time in the air, and part of the time out of the water. The top of the limestone fortress has a trapdoor with two plates that revolve to open and close. When the tide goes out and the barnacle is exposed in the air, the trapdoor closes and the animal sleeps inside its airtight prison. When the currents run over the barnacle, as the tide rises, the door opens and out come twelve feathery feet. The barnacle, more or less standing on its head, is in a good position to kick food into its mouth.

Although barnacles are fixed to a spot and unable to swim or walk, they do arrange to go on worldwide travels by cementing themselves to ships and whales. Sometimes they get about by hitching themselves to crabs or jellyfish.

MANY LITTLE WORLDS

Along the beaches there are many little worlds carved out by the winds and waves. Up among the high, dry sands, little beach fleas skip and feast among decaying seaweeds and dead animals cast up by the last storm. Somewhere along the beach, just beyond the highest waves at low tide, is a scattering of periwinkles, like dark gray pebbles, shut tight to keep the moisture in their shells, waiting for the tide to bring water again. Near these you may see hundreds of blue mussels, uncovered by the retreating tide, attached to rocks that are now sunsplashed, also waiting for the sea.

Down by the water's edge the waves bring in little sandbugs, which dig like sixty into the wet sand as the water slides away. A bubble popping out of the sand as a wave passes may tell of a clam at some secret business a few inches below. Wade out into the shallows and watch for a small spiraled shell—the remains of a long-dead sea snail—jerking through the water, propelled by a little hermit crab that will use it for his home until he needs a larger one.

Where the beach is always under water, the bottom may be covered with little boatshells, and big moss-covered whelks may be dimly seen here and there. Here, too, you may see the waving tentacles of a sea anemone, a calico crab scooting away from you sideways, or an eel rippling away into the green shadows.

Sunny tidewater pools are filled with seaweeds, mussels, starfish, crabs, and snails.

Every level of the seashore, above the waves and below them, has its own particular kind of small cities, some in view and some out of sight, where animals and plants have found just the homes that suit them, and where they go about the business of living as they have for a million years.

The Big Swamp

In the southeastern part of our country lies a mysterious region, neither land nor sea, hidden under a canopy of tangled trees. These trees, with leaves like feathers, stand on swollen bases in glassy-quiet water. Beardlike gray streamers hang from the branches, and little wooden projections from the tree roots, some rounded like knees, thrust up above the water. In the dim light the scene suggests a weird, haunted cave.

This is the Big Swamp, where numberless ponds are connected by twisting, unmapped waterways. Their banks are of treacherous black muck, out of which pour thickets of reeds ten feet high, and huge clumps of ferns. Everything is still—even the gray streamers, which the least whisper of wind would stir.

In this shadowy world time also stands still. Here is the threshold of land life, suggesting the earth of hundreds of millions of years ago, with its lush green ferns and strange trees—the damp, dim world where life first emerged from the ancestral waters.

Little islands called hammocks loom up here and there, like ships on a green sea. These are higher, drier ground—mostly dense scaffoldings of matted roots riddled with holes, teeming with life.

Here a strangling fig may drop its roots from a high perch in a palm tree. When these take hold, they swell up to form a tight sleeve around the trunk of the palm. At the same time the fig sends its leaves above the palm, cutting off sunlight. The palm dies, but the tough cylinder of the strangling fig still stands—a fake tree harboring deadly diamondback rattlers in its hollow where the palm tree has decayed.

Here, on the hammocks, grows the siren of trees, the gorgeous poison wood. Its red bark is exquisitely smooth, the yellow and white wood is as beautiful as any wood on earth, and its heartwood is mottled with green and gold. But the sap contains a burning poison.

The thick trunk of gumbo limbo, with red-brown bark that looks like a bad sunburn, undulates horizontally through the weird thicket like a huge fire hose.

Myriads of burrows within the root tangles are the hiding places of animals. Playful otters have a happy hunting ground under the glassy surface of the swamp. The raccoon, too, finds the hammocks a wonderful retreat.

MASKED GENTLEMAN

The raccoon, a gentleman despite his black mask, can easily handle a diamondback, and the snake has learned to stay clear when the gentleman is house hunting. By night the raccoon climbs high in a mastic tree to pick fruits like little olives, gummy to chew on and with a pleasant acid tang. Just before sunrise he descends to the water's edge to pounce on a frog, trap a fish in the shallows, and turn over rocks to catch water insects and snails. He cracks the shell of a snail like a walnut, and lets the soft body slide down his throat as dessert.

One flat stone turned over by the 'coon reveals a beautiful ringed snake, the animal counterpart of the poison wood. Most of its body has broad black and red rings separated by yellow rings, the tail being yellow and black, and the snout black. It is the coral snake, the most deadly reptile in our country. Its venom paralyzes the nerve centers and kills faster and more surely than the venom of any other reptile. But it is slow-moving, and by the time it is ready to strike, the raccoon is crunching snail shells a few stones away.

MOCCASINS AND DIAMONDBACKS

At sunrise, a water moccasin, the most dreaded snake of the swamp, comes to loiter

The painted turtle, one of the most familiar citizens of the swamp, has 250 million years of reptilian ancestry behind him. These turtles sunbathe in groups, on logs and rocks, and on the leaves of water plants.

The alert, intelligent raccoon washes his food when near water. He eats fruit, fish, meat and grain.

at the water's edge. He may coil up invisibly in a clump of grass, waiting for young rattlers, coral snakes, otters, muskrats—any prey at all. Just before striking, this four- to five-foot reptile lifts its triangular head and opens its mouth, which is white inside, like cotton. A creature that sees this yawn, close up, is in danger.

This water moccasin, or cottonmouth, may stay almost submerged, waiting for a frog or fish, but there is no telling where he may be hiding to open his mouth in a deadly yawn.

The diamondback is another creature that is at home in the hammocks. Not only is it the biggest poisonous serpent of our country, but it ranks high on the list of the deadly snakes of the world. Secure in its sheer power and size, it may grow to a length of eight or nine feet. Its enormously thick, muscular body does not have to coil for striking, but can flash out from a looped position.

This rattler is the more terrifying when it moves in a straight line. Most snakes must travel with a looping motion. Diamondbacks can do that too, when in a hurry, but when sneaking up they can advance as straight as an arrow, like the regal pythons of India and the huge boa constrictors of the tropics. Back-slanting scales on the belly catch against the ground and prevent any backward motion.

Animals of the Big Swamp hammocks lead peaceful lives on the whole. They do not collide on trails; trails are few and short, private roads from doorsteps down to the water's edge. Where there is muck among the roots, otters sometimes build toboggan slides, on which they shoot down into the water, again and again.

The Big Swamp, where good-natured raccoons and otters live next door to thieves and murderers, is like an enormous apartment house, with dens above and below and all around in the tangle of roots. But the heart of the swamp is down among the jungle of ferns and reeds.

The bullfrog's voice is the biggest part of him. Hunted by fish, snakes, and mammals such as the raccoon, he must be alert and agile. His big, popping eyes can detect danger behind him as well as in front. One good spring with his long legs usually carries him to safety.

THE REED-WALKING BIRD

The stillness of the steaming inner swamp is broken by a shrill scream, then a few harsh, squeaky notes. As the sound dies away, a limpkin bird, unconcerned at the dreadful noise it has just made, turns to picking little apple-like things from the curving reeds.

These are giant snails which have come up out of the muck to lay rows of little pink eggs high on the reeds. The giant apple snail has a powerful lung that extends half the length of her coils; she does not have to stay under water and breathe with gills, as many snails must. She has a strong shell with a heavy door that she can slam if danger threatens. Certainly she and her eggs should be safe on the high reeds. What animal, except the giant snail, could climb a frail, swaying reed?

But the limpkin knows what the reeds mean —dinner. It drops down easily among them. With its long toes it seizes a bunch of reeds at each step and walks around as though on stilts, swaying halfway between water and air as it picks off the apple snails.

The tree frog (left) is a vivid green, since it has just hopped out from its hiding place in the foliage of the tree. But after resting a few minutes on the gray bark, its skin turns a mottled gray (right) leaving the frog camouflaged and almost invisible—one of nature's many miracles of protective coloration.

THE MONARCH OF THE BIG SWAMP

On a calm, warm night in spring, the inner swamp is startled by a sound more weird than the limpkin's. It rumbles across the ponds and muck; it resounds among the animal apartments up in the hammocks. It is the breeding boom of the big bull alligator, whose kind roamed the swamps a hundred million years ago.

The ancient amphibians only partly succeeded in living on land. They spent half their lives breathing with gills under water. But the

The diving spider is an animal that must breathe air. Yet it builds its home underwater. The pictures above show how the spider swims up to the surface, catches an air bubble between his hind legs, and carries it down to his underwater nest. In this way he can store enough air to last for weeks.

ancestors of the alligator developed real lungs, and legs directly under the body—pillars to stand on and for running, with stomach off the ground. The alligator can run fast if he wants to, but he is lazy.

The front end of the alligator projects far out beyond the front legs, and the rear, far out

In the shallow waters of the swamp, one of the busiest animals is the stickleback. The stickleback, of course, is a fish, not a bird, yet its eggs are laid in a nest of twigs and grass. The male drives the female away to keep her from eating the eggs.

behind the back legs. Both ends are heavy and powerful. The thrashing tail end breaks the bones of the victim, and the mouth end holds and eats him.

The alligator doesn't go hunting. He just holds still, the water washing over his back, looking like a log. His nostrils and eyes look like bumps on a sunken log where branches have broken off. Thus he rests for hours, his eyes on the water's edge where all sorts of animals come sooner or later. Raccoon, otter, muskrat, lizard, snake, turtle, wading bird—an alligator will eat anything.

The eating of almost everything alive, big and small, bones and all, is made easier by the alligator's double stomach. This is a crop-and-gizzard arrangement like a bird's. Also like birds —which evolved from flying reptiles—the alligator swallows pebbles to help grind up fur, feathers, bones, shells, and teeth.

The great jaws open like a chasm, and down go fish, lizards, turtles, snakes. When the giant jaws clamp shut, they cannot be pried open even with a crowbar.

Sometimes the alligator takes a deep breath, closes his ear flaps, shuts off his nostrils, and sinks to the bottom. Warm-blooded animals need a lot of oxygen to burn fuel and keep their temperature up. But the alligator, with blood at about the same temperature as the air or water surrounding him, gets along on very little oxygen. He can stay under water for five hours. There it takes little energy to swing one's tail, float, swim, and tiptoe around.

Like a shadowy submarine the alligator seeks turtles and crabs, schools of darting little fish, or a big fish—different fare from the open-air menu of otters, raccoons, birds, and—with luck—rabbits and skunks. Under water, the otter is in no danger, because he is a remarkable acrobatic swimmer—almost impossible for any reptile to catch.

When hunting fish in schools, the alligator simply opens wide his huge jaws and, with a wave of his mighty tail, thrusts his body forward. His mouth is a collecting basket. Since water forced down his throat could drown him, his tongue wads up to close his throat when his mouth opens under water.

The alligator is happy to stay down for hours, but he often climbs ashore and, with muck dripping from his legs, goes for a walk. Soon he may lie down in the grass. In sunlight his pupils are narrow slits, and he looks sleepy. (His eyes round out only at night.) But beware an alligator "asleep" in the sun! As the sun warms him, he gets restless and hungry.

The alligator's scooplike lower jaw turns up at the rear, suggesting a smile. When the mouth opens slightly, at the prospect of good eating, long rows of teeth show and the smile becomes broader. Altogether the alligator is an amusing sight, except for anyone who gets too close to the smile.

Mother alligator, a true land animal, takes a walk when she wants to lay eggs. Finding a sunny spot, she sweeps together masses of leaves, grass, twigs, moss, and muck with her tail, and builds a heap two or three feet high and six feet across. She deposits a few dozen eggs, sweeps the trash over them, crawls over it all several times, and lets the sun do the hatching. Father never shows up, but mother stays in the vicinity. During the sixty days it takes the eggs to hatch, she may have to chase away snakes, skunks, and raccoons, which are drawn to alligator eggs as though by magnets.

One day there is a faint, high-pitched squeaking in the trash heap. This is music to the mother alligator, because it comes from the insides of the eggs. In a few hours the egg shells break, the mother alligator opens the nest, and out scramble the little alligators. These eight-inch babies have been coiled up in three-inch eggs. It must feel good to unwind.

THE MANGROVE

The Big Swamp is framed with beaches, shallow water, and mud flats wide open to the sky.

The fox snake lays its eggs in rotted logs, and feeds chiefly on rats.

Here are wide bayous on which soft green cushions float. These are thickets of mangrove trees, magicians of the plant kingdom.

Mangrove roots sprout from upper parts of the tree like ordinary leaf-bearing branches. The roots plunge straight down through the salt water and bury themselves in the greasy white mud. As they grow, they weave a basket under the mangrove tree that holds it well above water.

The mangrove does not scatter its seeds as other plants do when they put them into fruits, nuts, and berries or design them to be carried by wind. Such seeds would land on the salt water. So the mangrove starts its seeds growing up in the air. When a root has grown about a foot long, it drops off into the water. Like a little boat it floats off, its keel—the long root—keeping it upright. Sooner or later, the boat enters water less than a foot deep. The root touches bottom and catches hold. Another mangrove begins weaving its basket in the bayou.

The dragonfly (or "darning needle") is an expert flyer of the darting sort. Some have magnificent colors. This insect begins life underwater as an egg, hatches as a nymph, and finally crawls out of the water to dry off and start a winged life in the air.

SCALES AND FEATHERS

A brightly lighted outer swamp surrounds the dim mazes and hidden dens of the inner swamp. Here, in the outer swamp, standing in the shallow water or on the mangrove cushions —are the wading birds and water birds.

Ancestors of the alligator—grinning monarch of the inner swamp—led the parade of animals onto land. Ancestors of the big birds of the outer swamp conquered the air in another great adventure of life.

A pair of otters frolic in the green underwater world. Known for their playfulness, otters also are quick, deadly hunters. Their diet ranges from snakes and insects to rodents and birds.

Nature was no more satisfied to be bound to the land than to water. Flying is easier, smoother. Gliding, soaring, and diving are like swimming—the earliest form of locomotion. No wonder living things, having conquered land, attempted the air, where highways lead over the earth in all directions.

A hundred million years ago the reptiles tried to fly and succeeded in developing some heavy, crude pilot models. In some reptiles the fourth finger of each forelimb grew long and slender, and a thin light membrane formed between this finger and the side of the body. When the creature lifted its arms, it had an enormous wingspread—perhaps twenty feet. But the *pterodactyl* (Greek for "wing-finger") was no bird; its body was covered with scales, not feathers. To take off, it may have required a fast run and a tremendous leap. It may have launched itself from cliffs.

The key to the conquest of the air was the change of scales into feathers. The shaft of a feather is horny and tough like an elongated scale, yet hollow and thin and light. On this is mounted the lightest of fabrics, like silken threads hooked together—a tough yet almost weightless sail. Just as reptile scales can be swung open and closed, so feathers can be manipulated. Wing feathers can be spread for a broader soaring surface, pulled together for a greater speed, or adjusted to air currents for a light-footed landing. Feathers of a bird in flight are always in motion, according to flight conditions and the flight plan. Feathers can be folded close to the body to give off heat, and fluffed to save body heat. When feathers are oiled, they make a fine waterproof covering.

Other changes, too, were needed to turn reptiles into birds. Bodies had to be balanced differently, made smaller, given more strength per pound of weight. Hollow bones and powerful muscles for the breast were needed. Tremendous power was needed to drive wings, and heat to keep the animal's temperature at 104 degrees or more in water or in cold air. Hence birds' hearts work at high speed—hundreds of beats per minute. Yet, oddly, the reptile still lingers in bird blood: some birds, such as the

The flamingo rests comfortably on one leg, and when that gets tired, the other leg will take over. Its long legs enable the bird to wade into deep water in quest of food. The long, flexible neck allows the bird to reach down into the water, dredging for shellfish with its head held upside down. It also allows him to preen any part of his body with his bill.

robin, are born cold-blooded, and take days to warm up. Other birds, such as the chicken, are born warm-blooded.

The first feathered flyer, called *Archaeopteryx* ("ancient bird"), turned up in the middle of the Age of Reptiles. It had a long, reptile-style tail, with feathers sticking out on each side, and its eyes were set in its head like a reptile's. It had the teeth and ribs of a reptile. But the wings were birdlike.

Quick-darting, short-winged little songbirds were still millions of years in the future. Meadows blanketed by seed-bearing wildflowers and grasses, and forests of broad-leaved trees for insects to feed on—these still did not exist, and it takes myriads of seeds and insects to fuel modern songbirds. Ancient birds, therefore, had long legs and necks, and looked for their food mostly down in the water. Shellfish, crabs, fish, frogs—all sorts of food were to be had for the taking by reptiles and reptile-like birds, just as they are today for the waders and water birds.

LONG NECKS AND THIN LEGS

The long-winged birds still haunt the beaches, shallow water, and mud flats of the outer swamp. They help turn this living place under the wide open sky into a fairyland of color and design.

First prize for being the most astonishing and beautiful bird goes to the flamingo, who owns the longest and thinnest neck and legs in the bird kingdom. He swims through the air with restful rhythm, a gorgeous pink against the blue sky. His neck is so long that it must be carried with an S-curve sharper than the curves of a mountain road. The body, a little larger

than a football, is lifted high on slender stilts, which prance through the water softly. When taking a step, one leg bends at the ankle in the middle of the leg, the foot comes straight up, the toes point straight down, and there is hardly a ripple. Two sharp eyes are searching the bottom, and the least ripple or stir of mud would blur the view.

This bird is flexible in every part, quick to assume different shapes and sizes. When standing or wading he makes a vertical design, with the stilts straight up and the neck winding down. When flying, he becomes a horizontal line. His long legs, instead of folding under the fuselage like those of so many other birds, are stretched at full length straight out behind, while the long neck is thrust forward like a javelin. Legs and neck are the same length, balancing the buoyant body as the flexible wings beat steadily as pendulums. The flamingo does not swoop and dive: he flies only to go somewhere; all his hunting is done wading in shallows. Neither does he wheel suddenly. This magnificent flying machine curves widely into the wind for a gentle, silent landing on tiptoes.

Why is the flamingo such a bright pink or, sometimes, flaming red? Most animals hide from enemies by blending with their surroundings. They go through life inconspicuous and generally unseen—not waving bright banners. The answer is the same as to the question "Why are leaves on some maple trees red in the fall?" The answer is—"Why not?"

Flamingos fly mostly at sunrise and sunset; then they make black silhouettes against the sky. Actually, these wonderful birds need no colors to hide them. Eagles and hawks hunt things that run in grass; pelicans and herons do not attack other birds on the wing, but pursue seafood in deeper water. Nothing competes with the flamingo for his chief item of food—little snails buried in the mud. Other birds have the wrong kinds of bills for dredging up snails.

So this gorgeous bird can be gorgeous in safety. And this is a special advantage, because flamingos are sociable. They nest in mud towns and fly in flocks. Since they can see each other's bright plumage far away across the hunting flats, they can get together when it is time to go home.

THE MAN-O'-WAR BIRD

Outward bound from the top of a mangrove to the open sea, the mighty man-o'-war bird may cross the bows of the flamingo. But he is looking for pelicans or boobies.

A booby may have just completed his great stunt. From ninety feet he spots a fish in deep water, and trailing his wings plummets straight down. Going under the fish, he zooms up,

A group of solemn spoonbills, noted for their delicate pink hues, gather for a fishing party. The broad bill, from which the bird gets its name, is useful for shoveling up its food, which includes small fish, shellfish, water insects, and frogs.

The great blue heron is the largest of the herons. It stalks through the marshes on its long legs, spearing frogs, fish, and snakes with its long, pointed bill. Sometimes herons eat mice and insects. They gather in colonies, preferring to build their nests in tall trees—as shown here—or high on rocky cliffs.

The common gallinule is another marsh bird, fond of walking on the muddy flats and through the swamp grasses in search of leaves, roots, seeds, and insects. Its nests are built on the ground or in low vegetation bordering the swamp. Since the gallinule is not shy, it is easily observed; and is found in nearly every part of the world.

working both legs and wings, and catches the fish from below. The fish could well be surprised to find himself seized from below by a bird that was up in the sky a moment ago.

All this, however, is no use to the booby when the man-o'-war heaves into sight. This dark giant with the bent wings buzzes the booby—carefully, because he cannot risk getting hurt. He does not rest on water; his magnificent wings are not oiled, and he would be helpless if they got wet. The booby, which does not know the raider's weakness, is so scared that he drops the fish. Whereupon the bird that can't catch fish under water swoops

quickly below the booby and catches the fish in mid-air.

Let the flamingo have first prize for javelin-straight flying, but man-o'-war is the soarer. His body is light, about three and one-half pounds, and his wingspread seven feet. His feathers constantly feel the wind. Sliding on invisible currents, knowing their direction and strength, he traces beautiful designs against the sky—wide curves and circles and loops—without the flap of a wing. His contour feathers keep spreading and closing, and the long tail keeps working. So perfect is his control that man-o'-war can glide down to the water and pluck a fish off the crest of a wave without wetting a feather. He does that if he has had no luck finding a booby to scare, or a pelican from whose huge beak he can snatch a fish so neatly.

The pelican beak, with the skin bag dangling below it, is a fisherman's net and creel. Pelicans may fish by plummeting down like the booby or by swimming like a duck and scooping in fish with the long, deep-reaching bill. A pelican, with bones big and hollow and filled with air, and air pockets under his skin, floats like a cork. When he has scooped fish into his three-gallon pouch, he rises on an eight-foot wingspread and, with slow flaps, bears the heavy market basket home.

Little pelicans show their heads above the nest as dinner approaches. To their delighted "uk-uk-uk" their parent wisely replies "oke-oke-oke." The next minute there's a free-for-all, with each youngster trying to get more than its share, and with heads and necks plunging out of sight down the throat of the parent.

The heron's straight and sharp beak is perfect for spearing fish. The flamingo's is bent down almost at a right angle in the middle—just as it should be when the bird's head is upside down, at the end of the hose neck, when he is digging for snails. It is a perfect clam-digger's fork. But how the flamingo gets the snails up the hose into its stomach is anyone's guess. Perhaps he moves them up by working the throat muscles. This is just another mystery of the Big Swamp.

This noisy pelican fledgling is waiting in its nest of sticks, until its parents come to feed it live fish from their pouches. Pelicans like to live in bands, and even go fishing in groups, forming circles around schools of fish, herding them together and scooping them up in their huge, curved under-bills.

The nest of the redwing blackbird is built of reeds and grasses, and located on the ground in marshy meadows and swamps. Their blue eggs are partially camouflaged by brown speckles. The birds live in large flocks except while raising their young. Males are black with red wing-patches; females are a dusky brown.

Most of the time, the lion is quiet and dignified, as one would expect a monarch to be. He is very much like a large, contented house cat, enjoying nothing more than to lie in a comfortable heap, drowsing away the hours and blinking thoughtfully at goings-on around him.

Jungle, rolling hills, and white-crowned, majestic mountains are all part of the varied landscape of mysterious Africa. This is Mount Kilimanjaro.

Mysterious Africa

FAR away, beyond the curve of the earth, a huge block of granite—a section of the earth's crust—is lifted about a mile above sea level. This block, straddling the equator, makes a plateau known as the high plains of eastern Africa.

The plateau is broken by a diagonal crack twenty miles wide and three thousand feet deep. It has been punctured by a few volcanoes with high peaks, now white with snow, and shoulders hundreds of miles across. So vast is the granite block that the mountains are only isolated landmarks.

On top of the plateau, vistas of red grass are peppered with yellow rocks and thorny green acacia trees. Termite nests thrust gray cement fingers above the grass. Gullies fan out with secret trails, and scattered water holes sparkle here and there. White peaks float high in the purple air like pictures in a fairy story. In midday the sun blazes straight down. At night the stars and the moon are overbright in the clear air of the heights.

But the most astonishing thing about this plateau is the story of its animals.

RETREAT FROM THE ICE AGE

Once upon a time a vast variety of animals ran and jumped, roared and charged, snorted and fled over all the continents. America, Europe, and Asia were the homes of elephants. Rhinoceroses plunged through thickets as far north as the arctic. Lions and leopards stalked across Europe and Asia. Wart hogs built their villages in England. Giraffes browsed in the tree tops of Greece and China. Wild horses dashed over the plains of America.

Lands and seas were different in those days. America and Asia were connected; so were Africa and India. The Sahara, now a desert, was then green and fertile.

But conditions changed. Land bridges between the continents sank, or the continents drifted apart. Areas to roam in, as big as continents, were divided as the Rockies, Alps, and Himalayas rose higher. In northern Africa the grassland and shady groves, crossed by animal trails, turned into sandy desert.

Competition for food in the animal kingdom became more savage, and the animals had to fight to live. Those that ate the flesh of other

The lioness is a powerful, expert hunter, and the contented mother of a well-behaved family. Later, the male cubs will have a shaggy mane and a tufted tail.

animals became expert stalkers and hunters. Some mammals ate only plants, but to survive, they needed sharper eyes, longer ears, and faster feet. A few animals ate both plants and flesh.

Wonderful runners and jumpers developed. Teeth, claws, tails, and legs changed. Eyesight improved. Noses lengthened and were even pulled out to become trunks. Necks also became astonishingly long, as in giraffes.

Then lands in most of the world grew colder. Animals perished or retreated before the creeping glaciers of the Ice Age. But the high plains of eastern Africa, straddling the equator, were a refuge in the chaos of the Ice Age. As the animals retreated south before the ice, they were funneled into mid-Africa.

They came from the north and the east. On the high plains they found rolling grasslands to graze on, dry gullies to hide in, parklike groves for dozing in the heat of day, piles of stones for lookouts and dens, jungles with trees for safety, and water holes for all. It was a perfect place for the refugees of the primeval world.

Then another great geological event happened. With the breakthrough of the Mediterranean at Gibraltar, the rise of the Atlas Mountains, the creation of the Sahara Desert, and the separation of Arabia from Africa, the big continent with the animals on the high plains was cut loose from the rest of the world—by a sea of sand on the north, and by seas of salt water in all other directions.

The lioness leaves her cubs long enough to take a quiet walk and a refreshing drink at the water hole.

KING OF BEASTS

A great variety of animals live together on Africa's high plateau—but how can this be? Why don't bigger ones kill smaller ones, until only elephants and rhinoceroses are left? Somehow they have been sorted out by the ages, and organized to carry on life together.

Here on the African plateau, the lion is truly the king of beasts. Because of his great strength and noble bearing, almost all the animals show him tremendous respect. Only the giants, the elephant and the rhinoceros, ignore him.

In daytime the lion is lazy, sleepy. He hunts only at dusk and in the night. Then his great roar signals the start of the hunt. The herds are alerted, keyed up, ready to run. Animals at water holes stop drinking. If the lion shows up to take a drink, he has the place to himself. The others will return when he departs.

Why does the lion roar when about to kill? Perhaps because his lioness often does the killing. She has sneaked up on the other side of the herd, about a mile away, and his roar will drive the prey toward her. Sometimes he roars after making a kill—perhaps just to let off steam. Or the roar may be part of a warming up for a supreme effort. Animals bark, bellow, and howl for many reasons, but the lion's roar usually means he is hungry or angry.

In the daytime, and any time he is well fed, the lion is mild, tolerant, and good-natured. He sits in a comfortable heap, paws extended to one side, like a big house cat. His lioness and children purr contentedly to each other. But the lion is also curious. He will stare with big eyes and get up and walk slowly to examine anything he doesn't understand. He is not easily upset. He seems always to be thinking things over.

He stands high, his mane waving in the breeze like a king's flag. But when he stalks, he crouches low, with elbows high and stomach to the ground, invisible in the grass. This huge, elastic body, over ten feet from nose to tip of tail, has mighty power in its steely muscles and tendons. But the lion exerts himself little. He may kill only once a week, to eat, and never for the fun of killing.

The lion lurks on the fringes of the herds, coming up on them with the feel of the wind on his nose. He focuses on one animal and stealthily approaches foot by foot. Suddenly comes the rush, a few giant bounds, and hurtling through the air is an animal projectile that never misses. The sweep of a giant paw breaks the backbone, or one front paw placed on the doomed animal's neck and the other around the face will jerk the head back and snap the neck.

The other animals are now safe. They may graze in peace. The lion is feeding.

A mother lion carries the remains of her kill to a more comfortable dining place in the shade. Four cubs trail her, while a fifth impatiently paces around the dinner.

An impala cautiously begins drinking at the water hole, ears tuned for the slightest sound of danger.

ANTELOPE HEADQUARTERS

The high plain is antelope headquarters of the universe. Here antelopes, running by thousands, form the largest herds. Here antelope horns become more astonishing than any other horns in the animal world.

Some horns rise from the top of the head and undulate backward over the shoulders. Others stand straight up—long, slender, and spiraling. Those of the hartebeest wave up from the top of his forehead. The eland wears a crown like curving, unraveling straps. The sable antelope holds aloft a pair of crescents. Most stately of all are the lyres of the greater kudu. Antelope horns are hollow, except for a bony core near the base from which they continue to grow as long as the animal lives.

The gnu looks like a bit of mixed-up evolution. His body is slender and long-legged like a horse's, his horns are short and heavy as those of an ox, his head and shoulders are massive with mane and beard like a bison's, and his motions are unique. He trots daintily on tiptoe, suddenly he wheels around, looks back, flourishes his long horse's tail, puts head down and seesaws on his front legs, kicks his heels in the air, and gives a snort that resounds with a metallic ring. After that he takes off with long, stiff-legged strides, hardly seeming to touch the ground. Gnus can travel all day at this trot.

If gnus in a herd notice a peculiar motion in the grass, or have a feeling that something is stalking them from a gully, they halt and have a good look around. The leader heads toward the danger, followed by the herd in single file. When all are facing in the same direction, they stop. If the marauder is sighted, it is gnu custom for two of the biggest males to warm up for battle. They bow their heads and kick each other furiously for a couple of minutes as if to prove their ferocity and the appropriateness of their other name—wildebeests.

When animals herd together, it may be because they feel safer that way. A herd grazes, clatters over the plain, wheels in its course, and gets panic-stricken all as if controlled by one nervous system. It makes more noise, raises

When a giraffe drinks, he must do a split. Here, while two giraffes are drinking, the others keep watch in all directions.

One of the handsomest members of the antelope family is the graceful impala. The body is built for speed. As in many other hunted animals, the eyes are large, protruding, and set at the sides of the head, so that danger coming from practically any direction will be seen at once.

The grasslands – from the American prairie to the African veldt – support a rich variety of animal life.

more dust, looks more threatening than individuals. If it knew how to fight as an army, it could kill its strongest foes easily. But this it does not do. After all the display of mass strength, when the attack comes only one gnu fights; the others run away.

Does each survivor in the herd feel it has been saved by the crowd? All still appear to have a sense of security. True, one of their number is missing, but few saw it happen, and they don't call each other by name. They turn back to eating and drinking.

ANIMAL SKYSCRAPERS

From a tower—his neck—the giraffe looks down on the plain. He stares over the top of a tree, from which he has just lassoed a leafy branch with his eighteen-inch tongue. As he chews, his lower jaw goes round and round, as if being unscrewed.

The giraffe wants no part of the business of runners and hunters, but he may become involved if the lion begins thinking about having giraffe steak for dinner. Sensing danger, the stately, easygoing giraffes, perhaps a hundred strong, will take off and gallop for miles. They bring their hind legs in front of their forelegs, like coyotes and jackrabbits.

Strangely, the giraffe has the same number of neck bones as other mammals, including a mouse or a man. The miracle of the neck is achieved by lengthening each bone. In the same way, leg bones are lengthened. It all adds up to a towering creature that can enjoy fresh leaves and twigs, high on a tree, with little effort.

A giraffe makes good use of its fine view of the landscape. It gazes and gazes with big clear eyes, under beautiful heavy eyelashes. It takes note of any suspicious movement in the long grass; it sees down in the gully a tawny shoulder which is hidden from shorter animals. In fact, the giraffe has a reputation as a good lookout. When other animals see giraffes at a water hole, they come trooping over.

Nature made the giraffe's neck to stand up, not to swing all the way down. To drink, the giraffe must spread his legs far apart. Then his mouth can just barely reach the water. But in that awkward position he is helpless; he can't suddenly rear up and dash away. He has to pull his legs back slowly. So only one or two giraffes drink at a time, and the others keep a lookout while waiting for their turn.

With all his immense neck, the giraffe has no vocal cords. He cannot express feelings with a roar or a whinny. He can only stare at the world in silence. Except that sometimes after a long, long drink, air comes out of his mouth with a soft "*ah!*"

STRIPES AND BARS

Next to antelopes, the commonest herd on the mysterious plateau is composed of zebras. These look like little toy horses, the more so because their vivid stripes suggest a circus. Sometimes they trot along with their heads nodding in unison, wheeling and parading, as though showing off.

The stripes are a miracle of camouflage, for the critical time in the life of a zebra is the hour around sunset. That is when the dozing lion wakes up, stretches, utters a mighty hunting roar, and begins looking for dinner. Nothing will please the lion more than a zebra. But at this time of day the grasses and the clustered acacia trees throw long bars of sunlight and shadow across the ground. Where they fall, the zebra has only to stand still and vanish.

Shadows running through grass are broken, and so are the stripes of the zebra. The animal's bars all break through its outline. If they followed its outline, they would make the animal more conspicuous. The stripes cut over its back line and under its belly like hoops; they make rings on its neck and legs, and chevrons on its face. And this masterpiece of camouflage is, to repeat, most effective at sundown.

In daylight zebras are more conspicuous. The white fur between the dark stripes brilliantly reflects the light, and the animals look white on the plain. But the lion is not hunting now. When changing from one shady place to another, he may saunter casually through the herds. Then antelopes and zebras pause for a moment in their grazing, glance in the lion's direction, shift positions to give him a path, and calmly turn back to grazing.

THE TRUE NATIVE

The zebra, with its wonderful stripes, is a true native of the high plain. Lions, antelopes, elephants, giraffes—almost all other animals in the African ark—came from foreign lands, as well as possibly from Africa. The lion was well known in Greece, Syria, and Asia Minor. But it seems that zebras have never lived in any other place.

With giraffes as lookouts, zebras crowd into the shade of a tree to avoid the hot noonday sun.

This cheetah raced one of the fleet-footed antelopes of the high plain, and won; for the fast-moving, long-legged cheetah can streak after a victim at a speed sometimes reaching as high as seventy miles per hour. Notice the doglike appearance of this member of the cat family.

The first wild horses on earth, some fifty-five million years ago, were American. They were dog-sized inhabitants of the forests of North America before the Rocky Mountains were uplifted. These animals had four toes on each front foot, and three useful toes on each hind foot. As time went on, the number of toes decreased until thirty million years ago the foot of the horse had only three toes. Horses that run on one toe developed about twenty million years ago. This single toe became the hoof of the horse.

Legs on those American wild horses grew long and slender—giving better leverage for faster running. The hock of a horse, which looks like a knee turned backward on the hind leg, is actually an ankle. This shows how long and slender the foot is.

As ages rolled by, the miniature wild horses of America grew larger. When they migrated to Africa, they were probably about the size of wild asses which live in eastern Asia today. On the high plain some evolved into zebras—fat, striped, and with sleek hair. The burros and donkeys of our day, with their sharp little hoofs that can cling to stony paths up the sides of the Grand Canyon, are bred from the wild asses of Asia and North Africa. No tame animal has ever been bred from the zebra.

Far from being toy horses, zebras are pure wild animals. Nervous and alert, keen-eyed, they have a murderous kick. Efforts to tame them for harness and saddle are vain. Perhaps the individual is lonely and needs the herd. On the high plain they do always run in herds, whinnying together and kicking each other for a place at a water hole.

A peculiar layer of fat under the sleek zebra coat seems to make the animal cold-proof and heat-proof. Zebras are always plump. They drink a lot of water and never get more than five miles from a water hole. Other animals seem to know this and follow the zebras around when they are thirsty. The lion follows the striped herd, too, but only because he likes zebra meat for his dinner.

WORLD'S FASTEST RUNNER

While hunters are stalking the main herds, some superb races are taking place elsewhere. A small young antelope, a little zebra, or a rabbit, for example, will spot a cheetah and take off for dear life. The cheetah, spotted like a leopard, does not use the leopard's spring from a tree or rock onto the back of his victim. The cheetah depends on open-field running.

The cheetah is a cat, yet a little doglike. He sits high like a dog, with front legs planted like pillars. His claws are fixed like a dog's and cannot be retracted like a cat's. His legs are long, shoulders high, head small with piercing eyes,

Catching its breath after the chase, the big cat settles down to a dinner of fresh antelope meat.

and tail long. With a graceful combination of the long stretch of a greyhound and the springy swing of a monkey in full stride, this swiftest animal on earth in two seconds can get up to forty-five miles per hour, and with a *real* burst may hit seventy miles per hour. The little antelopes and the rest may, however, win the race if they get a good start. The cheetah tires fast.

TALKATIVE NEIGHBORS

A little way apart from the heavy drama of the African ark three astonishing animals are finding happiness—baboon, elephant, and rhinoceros. They are not bothered by the two big problems of hunters and hunted: how to eat and how not to be eaten. They find plenty of their kinds of food. Only one, the baboon, has an escape problem, and he has solved it in a peculiar way.

The baboon, being a monkey, is supposed to be a tree dweller. But African trees are the hunting place of the beautiful, slender leopard, which relishes baboon. So the baboon (no pea-brain he) left the trees and became a monkey that walks on the ground. Baboons moved into caves of rocky cliffs along streams, and into the

Two baboons, with the typical loops in their tails, go fishing in the shallows of an African stream.

piles of big boulders on the hills. Here they are safe while the leopard hunts among his tree branches in the moonlight.

Baboons live in clans of about fifty and are very sociable. They have the sharpest eyes on the high plain—eyes said to equal eight-power binoculars. When they see a trespasser, they all get mad and chatter and jeer.

Baboons look like long-nosed funny old men walking on all fours, but their stiff-legged, sidewise gait is fast. They sit down anywhere and amuse themselves by turning over stones, picking up the surprised ants and centipedes, and licking them off their fingers. Beetles and ants' eggs are especially favored, but these long-nosed fellows can live on all sorts of food, animal or vegetable.

When baboons are disturbed, they just talk loud and scamper off. Little baboons who can't keep up hitch rides on their mothers, where they look like bronco-busters. Or they grab the hair on Mother's stomach and hang on upside down.

THE LARGEST LAND ANIMAL

Behind the scenes the elephant is the most peaceful and happiest of the wild animals. He pays no attention to the others. Their hubbub does not bother him. The lion detours around the elephant, and the two seldom meet. The elephant's only encounter might be with a pack of wild dogs insane enough to gang up on him. In that event he curls his precious and delicate trunk up under his chin and, towering over the pack, lets them yap and dance around until they are tired and go away.

The elephant can stand still and reach far out in all directions with his trunk to collect an immense amount of food—about a quarter of a ton of green fodder every day. Without stretching his neck he can pick leaves almost as high as the giraffe can reach. With two little lips at the tip of his trunk, he pinches off tender twigs as delicately as though he were picking daisies.

The elephant has a way of reaching twigs and leaves beyond the reach of giraffes. If he takes a fancy to fresh leaves that are far up on a tree, he puts his forehead against the trunk and pushes. Down comes the tree—though its trunk may be two feet thick.

That elephant trunk, an elongated nose which coils and waves like a colossal snake, can reach down as easily as up. After a little plow-

Elephants are great waders. This one is perhaps looking for juicy grasses in the shallows along the bank.

The ridges on the underside of an elephant's trunk help in grasping. Not only males, but females too, have tusks, which are used mostly for rooting in the ground. Elephants are among the more intelligent mammals, but stories about their long memories have been exaggerated.

A herd of elephants wades into a stream to cool off from the hot African sun. One is taking water up into his trunk, and another squirts water into his mouth. Elephants do not drink through the trunk.

ing in the ground with the tusks, the elephant will pull up some tasty roots. If the tall grass around is going to seed, the trunk can touch the tassels gently, sniff in seeds, and then coil under and blow the seeds into the mouth. Or, if the tall grass has become dry hay, the elephant has huge teeth that act like grindstones. Like a long arm his trunk sweeps together an armful of grass into his eager mouth.

Though the elephant collects food on three levels, he needs a square mile to keep his stomach filled. So elephants sometimes have to bestir themselves. A herd may travel fifty miles in a night looking for water and trees, or reed pastures. Little elephants, which always trot along close to their mothers, are unable to go more than ten miles an hour, so mothers with children may get separated from the big old males. But elephants have a mysterious way of communicating and, somehow or other, they are able to find one another again.

The elephant's six-ton body is as well balanced as an antelope's. With its head, trunk, and tusks (perhaps three hundred fifty pounds of ivory) in front, the animal is balanced like a see-saw. When the trunk is held forward, the hind legs carry less weight and can push. The giant can move some twenty miles per hour, crashing through thickets as if they were tissue paper.

Sometimes elephants, usually very solemn, feel playful. If there is a steep, high bank by a

This elephant's trunk is curled around his next mouthful of grass. Despite his enormous strength, he does not kill to eat; he is a complete vegetarian. His animal neighbors have nothing to fear from him, except the risk of being stepped on.

Elephants sometimes strip whole branches from the trees while feeding, stuffing themselves with huge quantities of grass, fruits, leaves, and twigs—eating as much as half a ton of green fodder every day.

river, they stand on the edge to cave it in. Then they sit on their tails and toboggan-slide down in a cloud of dust. In the water they roll over and sink, putting up their trunks like snorkels to breathe through, with their heads under water. They suck up water and blow it over their backs and between their front legs at their stomachs. They love to roll in the mud.

JACKALS AND HYENAS

As grazing herds travel with the weather, back and forth over the high plains, with lions following, other animals are drawn into the strange procession. Among them are jackals and hyenas, seeking the carcasses which the lions leave. When the lion has eaten his fill, the jackals are first to close in.

The jackal hunts at night for small wart hogs, baby baboons, and rats. When he yaps at night at the big antelopes and zebras, perhaps he is calling a lion to come and do some killing.

The hyena is no hunter. Evil-looking and slow, he sneaks in at the end of a kill to finish whatever is left. Even the jackal hates the hyena, who comes in and pushes him aside. If tough hide, stringy hair, and skull and bones are all that is left, these suit the hyena. His powerful jaws and teeth will crunch the bones with loud cracking noises.

The hyena laughs at a carcass. His horrible laugh is that of a ventriloquist; it seems to come from the wrong direction. A ravenous pack of hyenas will produce the worst uproar on the face of the earth—a chorus of barks, squeals, hisses, wails, and shrieks. The lion pays no

A lion killed an antelope, fed, and went on. Now, the African wild dogs take their turn at the feast.

Although bad-tempered, and dangerous when he charges, the rhinoceros like the elephant is a plant-eater. He is active mostly at night. His eyesight is poor, but his sense of smell is exceedingly keen.

attention; but other animals may be scared away, for only the wild dogs are rough and tough enough to deal with hyenas.

THE WILD DOGS

The wild dogs, most ferocious animals of the African high plain, have big ears, long legs, and spots like a hyena's. They hunt in large packs, a leader out in front and the pack following in line about a half mile back. They hunt tirelessly day or night, not for food alone, like the lion, but with a lust for killing. Against them even the giant eland, weighing a ton, has no chance. It has been said that they will even gang up on a lion, driving his majesty from the kill. A pack may surround a lion and tear him apart, though not before some dogs have been torn apart first. The wild dogs are the lion's only real enemy.

The wild dog is a blood-thirsty villain, yet also a stylish and impressive animal. He swings into the chase with perfect teamwork, giving a

The rhinoceros is a leftover from prehistoric times. Large, armored bodies and little brains were more common among mammals then than they are today.

clear hunting call, *hooo-o! hooo-o!* like the wail of a bloodhound. He can outrun the fastest antelopes and zebras because he combines endurance with speed. As a killing machine he has few peers.

SULKY AND DUMB

If the elephant is happy, the rhinoceros is sulky and dumb. He has a very small brain in proportion to his body. He is left over from a bygone age of giant mammals which included, about twenty-five million years ago, the *Baluchitherium*, perhaps the biggest mammal that ever walked the earth. That monster rhinoceros was 34 feet long and 17¾ feet high. His shoulders were higher than the head of the giraffe is today!

The rhinoceros of the high plain is not greatly disturbed by animal hunters. He just sits around near his mudhole, surly, making sounds like a giant having bad dreams. He may stretch flat out in the mud like a pig, panting and foaming. But around sundown he scrambles to his feet and finds other rhinoceroses. If the night is moonlit, they squeal and snort, gambol, and boost, shove and try to upset each other. Some of them even bound into the air. It is disgraceful.

Intelligence, speed, and powerful horns characterize the African Cape buffalo. The base of the sharp horns forms a thick, bony helmet over the head.

A rhinoceros has a marvelous instinct for finding water. He seems to be able to smell it under the ground. Then he digs like a dog, sending the sand flying out between his hind legs. Other animals, even the elephant, get to depend on the rhinoceros as a water finder and a well digger. This is one of his contributions to life in the African ark.

The high plains of Africa—the greatest roaming ground for mammals in the entire world.

INDEX

Africa, 160-175
Ailanthus tree seeds, 110
Alaskan fur seal, 23-28, 29
Alligator, 151-153
Antelopes, 75-77, 164, 165
Ants, 104-106, 129-140
Arctic, 13-43
Auk, 43
Autumn, 97

Baboon, 169-170
Badger, 107
Barnacles, 146
Barrel cactus, 84
Bears, black, 45, 64-69
  polar, 13, 24, 28, 29, 37
Beaver, 51-56, 57, 58
Beavertail cactus, 93
Bees, 115-129
Beetles, 105
Big Adventures in Little Worlds, 95-147
Bighorn sheep, 46-49
Birds, 30, 35, 36-43, 72, 81, 83, 89, 90, 140-142, 156-159
Bison, 70
Black bear, 45, 64-69
Blackberry seeds, 112
Blackbird, 72, 140, 141, 159
Bladderwort, 109
Blubber, 19
Blue goose, 38, 39
Blue whale, 18
Bobcat, 86, 87
Booby, 158
Buffaloes, 70-74, 175
Bullfrog, 151
Butterflies, 95, 111, 114

Cactus, 82, 83, 84, 85-86, 87, 93
Cactus wren, 89
Canada goose, 43
Cape Buffalo, 175
Caribou, 32
Caterpillar, 144
Cheetah, 168, 169
Chickadee, 142
Chimney Rock, 76
Cholla, 85, 87
Cinquefoil, 17
Cobra plant, 108
Coconut palm, 110, 111
Coral snake, 149
Cormorant, 30, 43
Cottonmouth, 150
Cougar, 51, 61-63
Cowbird, 72
Coyote, 55, 58, 76, 77, 78, 79, 80
Crabgrass, 110
Creosote bush, 85
Crowberry, 20
Cuckoo, roadrunner, 89-90

"Darning needle," 154
Death Valley, 83
Deer, 32, 47, 62
Desert, 82-93
  Great American, 83
Diamondback, 150
Diving spider, 152
Dog, wild, 174
Dovekie, 43
Dragonfly, 113, 154
Duck, goldeneye, 40
Duck hawk, 40

Earthworm, 104
Eider, 42
Eland, 164
Elephant, 170-173
Elf owl, 83
Elk, wapiti, 49, 56-61
Ephedra bush, 85
Ermine, 34
Erosion, water, 98, 102

Falcons, 40, 81
Fawn, 47
Ferret, 107
Fires, forest, 103
  prairie, 72, 73
Flamingo, 155, 156-157
Fossils, 99
Fox, arctic, 24, 29, 31, 35
Fox snake, 153
Frog, 150, 151

Gallinule, 158
Geese, 38, 39, 43
Gila Monster, 88
Giraffe, 164, 166-167
Glaciers, 12, 14
Gnu, 164
Goat, mountain, 46, 50-51
Goldeneye duck, 40
Golden plover, 43
Goldfinch, 141
Gopher, pocket, 81
Grasshopper, 143
Grasslands, 166
Gray lizard, 90
Greasewood, 85
Ground hog, 107
Grouse, 80
Gulls, 30, 41
Gumbo limbo tree, 149

Hartebeest, 165
Heron, 158, 159
Horned lizard, 88
Hummingbird, 141
Hyena, 173

Icebergs, 12, 14, 21
Impala, 164, 165
Insects, 144

Jackal, 173
Jaeger, 43
Joshua tree, 87, 92

Kangaroo rat, 88, 89
King snake, 88
Kudu, 164

Lava, 100-101
Lemming, 31-36
Lesser snow goose, 39
Lichens, 17
Limpkin, 150
Lion, 160, 162, 163
Living-rock cactus, 85
Lizards, 88, 90
Mangrove tree, 154
Man-o'-War bird, 157-159
Maple tree flowers, 145
Maple tree seeds, 110
Mauna Loa, 99
Measuring worm, 146
Mesquite, 84
Milkweed, 112, 113
Mole, 107
Monarch butterfly, 114
Mormon tea, 85
Moth, pronuba, 92
Mountain goat, 46, 50-51
  lion, 62
Mountain stronghold, 44-69
Mount Kilimanjaro, 101
Mule deer, 62
Murre, 42
Musk ox, 15-18, 19

Narwhal, 20-21

Oak tree, 113
Ocotillo, 87
"Old Man of the Mountains," 50
Orchid, 110
Organ-pipe cactus, 85
Otters, 25, 154
Owls, 35, 83

Pelican, 159
Pepsis wasp, 91-92
Peregrine falcon, 40
Petrified wood, 84-85
Phalarope, 43
Pigweed, 110
Pincushion cactus, 85
Pine tree flowers, 145
Pipewort, 20
Pitcher plant, 109
Plover, golden, 43
Pocket gopher, 81
Poison wood tree, 149
Polar bear, 13, 24, 28, 29, 37
Pollen, 112, 114, 115, 117, 118, 119
Poppies, 93
Prairie, 70-81
Prairie dog, 77, 78, 79, 80, 81, 106
Prairie fires, 72, 73
Pribilof Islands, 23
Prickly-pear cactus, 85, 87, 93
Pronghorn antelope, 75-77
Pronuba moth, 92
Ptarmigan, 37
Puffin, 43

Queen Anne's Lace, 114

Rabbits, 37, 88, 106
Raccoon, 149, 150
Rainstorms, 102
Rattlesnake, 90
Red clover, 110
Rhinoceros, 174, 175
Ring-billed gull, 30, 41
Ringed snake, 149
Roadrunner cuckoo, 89-90
Rocky Mountains, 44
Roots, 102-103

Sable antelope, 164
Sagebrush, 85
Sage grouse, 80
Saguaro cactus, 82, 83, 86, 93
St. George, 23, 28
St. Paul, 23, 28
Saxifrage, 17, 30
Seals, 23-28, 29
Sea Otter, 25
Seasons of the year, 95-98
Seeds, 101, 109
Sharp-tailed grouse, 80
Sheep, bighorn, 46-49
Sidewinder, 89, 90
Sitka spruce, 44
Skua, 41
Snails, 151
Snakes, 88, 89, 90, 104, 149, 150, 153
Snow goose, 39
Snowshoe rabbit, 37
Soil, 102, 104
Spiders, 91-92, 142-143, 152
Spoonbill, 156, 157
Spring, 96
Spruce, Sitka, 44
Squirrel, 66
Stickleback, 152
Stove Pipe, 83
Summer, 95, 97
Sundew, 108
Swamp, 149-159

Tarantula, 91-92
"Tarantula hawk," 91
Teddy-Bear cactus, 85
Tern, arctic, 38-42
Tidewater pools, 147
Timber wolf, 32, 33, 61
Tree frog, 150, 151
Trees, petrified, 84-85, 149
Tundra, 14, 20, 29
Turtle, painted, 148

Venus fly trap, 108
Volcanoes, 100-101

Walrus, 21-23
Wapiti elk, 49, 56-61
Wasp, pepsis, 91-92
Water erosion, 98, 102
Water moccasin, 149
Weasel, 34, 36, 42
Whales, 18-21
"Whistler," 40
White whale, 20, 21
Wild dog, 174
Wildflowers, 14, 93
Winter, 97, 98
Wolf, 15, 16, 17, 59
  timber, 32, 33, 61
Woodchuck, 107
Woodpecker, 89, 140-141
Worm snake, 104
Wren, cactus, 89

Yucca, 87, 92

Zebra, 167-169

C